CHILLIN IN NEGRIL

The Unofficial Negril Jamaica Travel and Party Guide

GEORGE F. FELDMAN JR.

All rights reserved. No part of this book may be reproduced in any form including any electronic or mechanical means, unless you're crazy enough to write a review.

Information in this book is without warranty, and the author is not responsible for incorrect or out-of-date prices and information.

This book is a work of fiction. All of the characters, organizations, events, hotels, people, places, and things in this guide are the products of the author's imagination or are used fictitiously.

This book is for amusement only. In no way should anyone try anything in this book. The author and publishers shall have no liability to any person or entity with respect to any loss or damage caused or allegedly caused directly or indirectly by the information in this book.

This book is for adults only. No one under eighteen should be reading this book! Use common sense! The author and publishers of this book are not liable for accidents or mistakes made on vacation in Jamaica or anywhere else!

All names, dates, prices, and other information in this book are only editorial opinion and not the views of anyone, except the author.

If the Jamaican Chamber of Commerce catches me, I'm done!

Trademarked names may appear in the guide and are used in an editorial fashion with no intention of infringement.

Accidents while cliff diving, snorkeling, drinking, eating or smoking strange plants, or consuming enough drugs to stop a bull elephant are not the fault of the author or publishers.

All the lawyers can go back to the golf course now.

Chillin' in Negril: The Unofficial Negril, Jamaica, Party and Travel Guide

Copyright © 2013 by George F. Feldman JR.
All rights reserved.

ISBN: 1484854446
ISBN-13: 9781484854440
Library of Congress Control Number: 2013908695
CreateSpace Independent Publishing Platform
North Charleston, South Carolina

Visit: chillininnegril.com
Back cover: The Fireman about to grill

Extra thanks to Travis Feldman for the support and technical help
Chillin' in Negril is Number One in the Twisted Travel Series (copyright 2013)
—and according to my wife, the last.

Guide and all photographs by George F. Feldman Jr. and George Feldman Publishing

DEDICATION

LONGEST EVER

This book is dedicated to the island of Jamaica and the beautiful folks living in and around Negril.

It is also dedicated to my family, whom I love dearly: my beautiful and very understanding wife, Lynn, and both my sons, Trey and Travis, my mother, sisters, and brothers, Eva, Greg, and Elizabeth, and their loved ones, plus all my cool little cousins and nephews, Karen and Lisa, Scott, Eva, Jillian, Jason, Johnny, and Laurel and Margarita; to all my Italian family; to my lifetime friends, Bobby Jones, Kevin Heffernan, Sam Harr, Mike Wilson, David Imel, Jim Maxwell, Brandon Reed and Della Marie, Cinnie Bash, Curt Hoagland, Scott and Betsy Boleman, Dr. Dan Shull, Pat Wagner, John and Linda Anderson, Curt and Mary Shields, Art and Ann Overmeyer, A.C. Paul and the Eagle, Ian Harris and Beverly Cox; to my Jamaican explorers and traveling companions from England: Jason Cosat, Dave Mekos, Terry Spurgen, Bill and Triesa Hodgson, Dale Avers, Barry Monschein, Rufus Hardeman, Tracy Sigler, Brittnay and Adrienne, Bud and Kathy Dawson; to my neighbor, Alan Buyers (Alien); to Ryan and Joni Neely; and the folks at Community Chrysler—every one of you better buy a copy of this book now that I stuck your name in it, so that's at least twenty-five copies sold! Sorry if I forgot anyone! Also, this is for my brother, Charlie, my dad, George Feldman Sr., Uncle Charlie Feldman, Gary Goddard, Norman Taylor, Julie Boller, and Tim Kemp—my good family and friends chillin' in heaven.

TABLE OF CONTENTS

DEDICATION III

INTRO 1

A WAY TO JAMAICA 5

SEVEN MILES OF SAND 17

CHILLIN' AT HEDO 33

BLOODY BAY 43

THE WEST END IS THE BEST END 49

PSSSST, GANJA! 65

BLOW YOUR MIND ON THE BEACH 81

ISLAND MUNCHIES GRILLIN AND CHILLIN' 89

SEX WAVES 101

CRIME AND COMMON SENSE 115

NATURE BOUND 121

WATTA... 125
ABOUT THIS BOOK!... 135

CHAPTER 1
INTRO

CHILLIN', MON!

Chillin' in Negril is your mental map to this crazy yet mellow island getaway. This rare and valuable guide will gently enhance your trip, with tips, pictures, and stories for getting your cool self a guaranteed outer-limits-reggae-induced-style vacation you've been imagining.

For those seeking a frosty travel experience, this could be it! Negril contains special vibes known only to exist in remote and spiritually sensitive fragments of the globe blessed by sun, sea, soul, ganja, and the assortment of amazing people who inhabit the gold, green, red, and black mystery that is Jamaica.

This isn't a guide to the secret gems of "the hidden Jamaica" that need a biplane to find. It's a guide to the simple, easy-to-find, very cool places that can be found by taxi, boat, or flip-flop power. Bouncing around Negril will keep your time here interesting and funky. Like financial advisors say, try to diversify…your vacation.

Negril is a tropical, sun-drenched, beer-sipping, laid-back, ganja-smoking paradise in close proximity to heaven. Sometimes it's a lunatic rolling around eating sand, talking to the air as he spins wildly, making a grab at your drink. Sometimes it's loud and crazy, as multiple reggae parties rock the beach at night, with people stumbling around higher than lab rats, creating a tropically charged sexual atmosphere so hot it forms a layer of molten glass on the beach. It's smoking ganja, watching bats fly by in a blur as the ocean laps into labyrinths of coral caves. It's munching on grilled lobster and jerk chicken by the cliff's edge, overlooking a crazy blue sea, waiting for the rare green flash of sunset, or getting naked in the hot tub with twenty-seven strangers at about one in the morning, or burning your back to a crisp, bright, lobster-tail shade of crimson as you pass out on the beach, or trying to consume all the Red Stripe on the island while jiving with street vendors and beach hustlers. It's walking down a road chewing sugarcane, cruising on a catamaran with insane party animals, or riding a horse on the beach. Negril can be a very cool place to hang out.

Browsing *Chillin' in Negril* will lead you off a rosy path into a jungle of experience, where things are an unpredictable, verdant mystery alongside an all-embracing exuberance that's the home world of lotus eaters and party animals of all types and strains. So read on, pilgrims. Jamaica awaits you. Welcome to paradise, mon!

THIS BOOK IS ADULTS ONLY!

Negril is not the best place for young children, unless you can go to an all-inclusive resort (AI) and hang. Really, how are you going to do anything with the kids around anyway? Soooo much more fun to leave them at home! If you bring kids, you may or may not be exposing them to a little more strangeness than you thought, so if you want to bring the rug rats, an AI might be your best choice. Although many brave and adventurous parents do it, if you're bringing children, I suggest that you avoid the beach over the cliffs, as there is little for kids to do, and the cliffs can be very dangerous. It's mostly an adult playground, and nowhere near any Disney theme parks. If you're bringing kids, do diligent, online research for child-friendly destinations.

CHAPTER 2
A WAY TO JAMAICA

THE TRIP

Off we go to Negril, where you'll have a blast visiting one of the coolest places on the planet.

First, if you realize now that getting there is only half the fun, you will increase your odds of a better trip. Airport parking, the TSA, customs agents, passports, luggage, and other passengers trying to carry everything they own in a tiny bag stuffed with souvenirs and airport food in the hustle of achieving objectives and intentions unknown to you—they're all part of the trip. It's just something you have to deal with—like being strip-searched.

Try to relax, and take all the weird circumstances you have to go through in stride.

Most airports have an amazing selection of bars and all manner of sports lounges surrounded by large flat screens blasting away the latest scores and serving overpriced drinks to anxious voyagers like you. Those tiny bottles on the plane may be able to help, and vodka tonics are a safe and natural cure for turbulence.

Jamaica's close proximity to the United States means that within hours, you can be lying out in the hammock with a Red Stripe in one hand and a dirty banana in the other, and all that hassle just melts away. If you're flying in from Canada, it's going to take a little more time and fortitude. Do your online research like a travel pro, and with just a little advance planning, you'll have an extremely cool adventure. With today's online access to every airline, travel site, resort, hotel, restaurant, and attraction, it's exceedingly uncomplicated to book your own travel. Here's what it takes to break out and get away to Negril, Jamaica.

PASSPORT FIRST

You should have one anyway. It's the preeminent form of ID and the only way you can get into or out of a free country! You must have a current passport to enter Jamaica from another country by air. If your background is clean as the driven snow and not slightly drifted (and if you are a citizen), you qualify for a US passport.

CHAPTER 2: A WAY TO JAMAICA

Your old traffic tickets or bad credit rating or tribal tattoos will not stop you from getting a passport, so off you go to the local post office with all the IDs you can muster. You should have original documents: a driver's license or other government ID, a one-inch-square picture of yourself, stamped birth certificates—no generic copies. It currently costs about $110.00, plus $25.00 for processing. All the information is now online, so you can do it all from the cozy confines of your abode. It will take the government passport office about four to six weeks to complete your application. If money's not an object and speed is, you can expedite your application through one of many government-approved sites and have your passport in twenty-four hours. A less expensive approach to getting your passport quickly is adding a sixty-dollar rush fee at the post office. Then it should arrive within three to four weeks—or sooner. It's good for ten wonderful years, so use it.

OK, once you've got your passport, autograph it in black ink, fill out the separate card, and cram it into your purse or wallet with the rest of the stupid cards you're forced to carry around. Write all the information on that card and keep it on your person with a black pen, so you can fill out your citizenship and entry cards on the plane.

A passport card has your passport number on it in case of emergency, or in case you ever lose the original. Keep them separate. A passport is one of the most precious assets you own. Protect it well from thieves and pickpockets because on black markets around the world, it's worth its weight in gold. You can't bend or deface it in any way. Find a passport cover and guard it at all times. Never pack it when traveling and keep it well concealed.

Stash all documents and ID where thieves can't get to them, like in your front pocket or a similarly well-hidden location.

It could be that your budget hotel won't have a room safe, so be certain your passport goes to the front-desk safe, or rent a safe-deposit box, even if there's an extra charge. If you lose it, or it's stolen while you're away, it'll become a nightmare, and you'll have to go right to a US consulate, government diplomatic service, or just swim out to sea.

ONLINE AND GO

There's a lot of competition in the travel industry. Airlines, resorts, travel sites like Expedia, Travelocity, and Kayak, and lonesome travel agents all want a shot at your hard-earned assets. You can do your own personal travel booking, and it's a trouble-free way to save some cash.

First, select your travel time and give yourself a little wiggle room—a few days if you can. Sometimes there's a vast price discrepancy, depending on the season. Also, the airport you choose to soar out of makes a monster difference in pricing and flight times, so search around. When using travel sites that combine hotels and flights (like Expedia and Travelocity), you must pay close attention to the first set of flight times the site will display. It may look

cheap, but it's a twenty-seven-hour flight with three connections. We'll see you next week! Mess around until you find the quickest flight, with no more than one connection to Montego Bay's Sir Donald Sangster Airport. Don't go too cheap; you want to reach your destination as fast as you can. These sites usually give you a discount if you book your flight and room together as a package deal. This can work out well to your advantage. It stops you from making separate bookings, and you'll have the company as your representative if something goes haywire with the trip. Almost every hotel and resort in the world has its own website now, as do all the places mentioned in the guide. You can always book directly with any property or airline. A week in Negril, including your flight plus a cool, rustic room by the sea, can (as of 2013) be had for about $650.00 and up, depending on season and choice of hotel. A special rate at an all-inclusive resort will start at around $1400, including flight, with price fluctuations depending on the season.

With so many options of where to stay and whom to book with, take your time and try not to rush your trip. Planning ahead can save money and brain damage. You can book up to a year in advance, or as little as two weeks.

If you don't have an Internet connection, you can go to most public libraries to hop online. If you don't want to hassle with it, there are still loads of travel agents out there.

DON'T FORGET TRAVEL INSURANCE!

Traveling in other countries will mean you are subject to the care, risk, and cost of another country's health-care system—or resort nurse. Injuries and death happen quite frequently on vacation, and smaller injuries, such as cuts and falls, are even more prevalent. People are constantly losing their minds from drinking too much and deciding it's time to ride a narwhale or to pick a fight with the biggest guy in the bar. Falling flat on your face in unfamiliar places—like the slick edge of the pool—and other silly accidents usually take place because folks are on vacation or spring break, showing everyone on Facebook what fun they're having.

Various accidents from car wrecks to hurricanes can impede any stay away from home, because fate (or destiny) happens all the time to everyone. Poor infrastructure, loose bricks on the pier, uneven walkways at the resort, a slippery deck on the boat, tainted food—if you can think it, it happens.

You have insurance at home to cover the expensive medical payments and unexpected craziness that happen every day, so common sense should tell you that you'll need it twice as much in unfamiliar territory. Don't make the common mistake of leaving the country without some good travel insurance just because you're twenty-six and bulletproof. Whether or not you ever need medical treatment while on vacation, travel insurance is worth every penny.

Imagine your traveling companion's surprise when he wakes up in a Jamaican doctor's office because he got extremely drunk and walked right into a pole, cracking open his head, spilling copious amounts of blood on the bar, and needing ten to fifteen stitches. It happens all the time. He'll be glad he's still alive, and when the bill arrives, he'll be grateful for the insurance. If the unthinkable happens, and a traveler is severely injured or killed, insurance plans will cover much of the cost of any emergency evacuation or return of remains. If your flight is cancelled ten times because of strange and unusual atmospheric disturbances, you have flight cancellation and interruption insurance to assist in paying for the additional expense. You'll even have coverage for lost baggage or equipment. Travel insurance—DON'T leave home without it!

Look online for travel insurance and use trusted companies like Travel Guard. Or you can purchase insurance with most travel sites when booking your trip. Check your own insurance company to see what, if any, coverage you have when out of the country. Search online for the best coverage for your trip, but whatever you do, make sure you get some insurance before you leave the country.

MI RIDE, MON!

Time to make a decision on travel arrangements to and from the airport! Don't waste your time with the resort or group bus, unless it's a free service that's included with your hotel package. It may take forever to get to your hotel while they drop off other passengers, and you don't want to waste precious vacation time stuck in the back of a hot, crowded minibus, sucking up diesel fumes, when you could be on the beach already.

Go online and search for a transport company or service to destinations in Negril and surrounding areas. When going to Negril, you'll need a ride from Sir Donald Sangster Airport to your resort or hotel in Negril, which is little more than an hour and a half in traffic. There are countless ways to get to your resort—taxi, bus, island hopper, motor scooter, or rental car for the brave and experienced.

Jamaicans drive, like the English, on the WRONG side of the road, so driving here is wacky if you're from the States. Be prepared to be entering the wrong side of the cab all week.

All-inclusive resorts may have a driver or bus for you. Check to see if it's actually free, or if the resort thinks it's doing you a favor. When you arrive, they'll be outside the airport gate with a company sign and are easy to locate, even in the confusion outside the gate.

Although prices change with the cost of living and fuel, as of 2013 you should be paying about $70.00 one way to Negril, but sharp negotiations with a taxi driver might get you there a little cheaper.

We recommend using Clive's Transport if it's your first trip; go online to www.clivestransportservicejamaica.com. Pay online or with cash when you arrive. This is a great service we always use when going to Negril. Clive's Transport can take you about anywhere in Jamaica, and they have a good, easy-to-navigate website with information on tours and places to go.

PICK IT UP AND LET'S GO PARTY!

Packing is easy for your vacation adventure in Negril. Having the time of your life doesn't mean taking much except basic beachwear,

money, and a don't-worry-be-happy attitude. You may have what's called a suitcase, for which the airlines will gladly charge you an extra fee of about twenty-five bucks. If you're getting away for a few nights, a carry-on is perfect, and it's free to drag with you.

If you're going on vacation for a week or so and your significant other is coming along, the reality is a two-suitcase trip. Great! You've got room for all the stuff you won't need and room for junk to take home.

Negril is one of the most relaxed, casual vacation destinations on the happy planet! You can be so informal, relaxed, and laid back here as to almost forget the clothing, and in a few spots, it's not necessary to wear anything, anyhow. Pack light if possible. It's less stuff to drag there and back. Pack according to your destination: some AIs have formal dress codes for the special restaurants, so check your resort website.

Naked (or as naked as the law allows) is more the norm along the beach: T-shirts, shorts, hats, bathing gear, little string things, flip-flops, beach shoes, and sunglasses. Don't be tempted to bring along clothes and outfits you never wear, thinking they will be perfect for vacation. They will end up in the bottom of your bag as deadweight. Let them stay at the bottom of your dresser and bring clothes you would normally wear. Think casual party time, Bob Marley T-shirts, and bikinis. Lotions, potions, sunscreens, insect repellent, and such are expensive on the island, so ram a quantity of personal care items into your suitcase. You can't do this with a carry-on bag because of the TSA's three-ounce rule for liquids. Go online to the TSA website first and read up.

Try this! Fling stuff in and out of your bag for a month until you get it right. Then take more clothes out and double your money.

TAXI TIPS

Taxi rides in Jamaica are a part of the fun and can be death-defying depending on the driver, day, and traffic. Prices are never set, and there are no running meters, just general guidelines, which can all be negotiated before you enter a cab. A cab ride around the Negril area should only be a couple of bucks as it's just a straight stretch of road. Locals cruise for only two dollars, so don't pay over five dollars for any ride around Negril. If your driver won't accept your price, just say OK and get another cab. There are thousands that cruise the area looking for riders. Most will take your offer.

Look at your driver first! If he's higher than a kite or drives a shitty car—pass. This is not a place to take chances in on the road.

Robot drivers are illegal taxis, and they are everywhere in Jamaica. Use a JUTA legal taxi only, with red license plates.

Taxis are everywhere and are continually honking their horns to see if you want a ride. There is no lack of transportation in this town. If you want a taxi just walk to the road and wave. Also, any gate guard at any resort or hotel in Negril will get you a taxi in about three seconds.

FIVE USELESS TIPS!

1. PACK LIGHT, AND DON'T FORGET SUNGLASSES.

2. DON'T BOTHER CONVERTING MUCH MONEY INTO J$ (JAMAICAN DOLLARS).

3. BRING PLENTY OF SMALL BILLS FOR SPENDING AND TIPS.

4. POTIONS AND LOTIONS ARE EXPENSIVE ON THE ISLAND.

5. LEGAL OR JUTA TAXIS HAVE RED LICENSE PLATES.

CHAPTER 3
SEVEN MILES OF SAND

FREE STUFF

Seven Mile Beach winds itself around a minute and striking segment of the western side of the island. It's the beach that put Negril on the map as a vacation destination. Fronted by AIs and smaller hotels, restaurants, and vendors of all things Jamaican, it beckons like an ancient sea siren calling for beer and grilled lobster with fresh-squeezed lime.

What was once home to the Arawak island peoples, as well as pirates, wenches, whalers, and smugglers, is now lined with places to party from dusk till dawn with reggae, ganja, half-naked vacationers, Rastafarians, and Red Stripe taking their places. Seven

Mile Beach is now lined with what seems like hundreds of places to stay, and almost every one has a restaurant or bar, so there are lots of choices about where you can consume rations and drink yourself into a state of hyper-induced love. Tiny grills and people selling whatever crawls or swims in the sea, or hangs from a tree, range the beach from end to end.

Everything can be found along the beach for sale, but the free stuff is always before you. The ocean's turquoise reflection blinds you with five shades of blue. Smells blast senses that you forgot were lurking in that biomass of sunburn you call your nose. There's an island vibe most particular to this part of the world, where you hear drums banging away in the direction you're going. With a light breeze wafting along the shore, you walk down the beach, avoiding the surf, watching your footsteps melt away like time itself. Raise a drink in salute to that majestic palm tree and its family of coconuts. Jah knows, free is good!

CHILLIN' IN NEGRIL

You're in Jamaica, mon! With a little fewer than a zillion hotels and resorts, from Bloody Bay to the end of Seven Mile Beach—and

CHAPTER 3: SEVEN MILES OF SAND

who knows how many scattered across the road and even more nestled among the cliffs at West End—the variety of cool places to stay is mind-blowing. Granted, there are many fantastic AIs here, but they are not the focus of this guide.

People love the all-inclusive resorts (AIs), and Negril is a great vacation spot, no matter where you stay. Resort chains dripping in  opulence and cozy love nooks are filled with weddings and honeymooners, because Jamaica is one of the most romantic tourist destinations in the Caribbean. A majority of these hefty and beautiful AIs are located around Bloody Bay, a large expanse of beach east of the regular seven-mile hustle. If you'd like to stay on the Bloody side but still want to avoid the AI scene, see our review of Our Past Time Hotel and Villas, an inexpensive and rustic hotel snuggled right up next to the big boys on the block.

There are heaps and mounds of information about these places online at TripAdvisor and in standard travel guides like *Fodor's* and *Lonely Planet*. Unfortunately, these spots often lack soul and show you a sterile version of the island. Of course, I'm not being fair because anywhere you stay will be better than six inches of snow and a median temp of fourteen-below in Michigan, or sloshing about in the muck of a weary, wet winter in jolly ol' England.

Here are a few groovy, mind-blowing places. These spots are selected because they are tons of fun to be at, because they come with astronomical recommendations, and because they allow you to leave that certain world behind, exchanging it for an alternative one: a stress-free, laid-back, serene zone of pure heliolatry, sun worship, and pleasure.

7-MILE BEACH FEELS LIKE 4-EVER

One of the best all-year-long parties is Seven Mile Beach, and that's where resorts, hotels, and hip bungalows snuggle up next to each other. This is where most visitors stay for insane fun while in Negril—right among the swaying palm trees, golden bits of sand, and pelicans foraging for their supper of needlefish and sea scraps.

Beach, boats, watercraft, restaurants, spas, T-shirts, bars, Jamaicans doing what they do, crazy parties, and ganja in the air all blend together to become a magic haze of amazing places to stay. The Moon Dance Villas are next to the Wild Parrot; Legends is next to Hidden Paradise, and Kuyaba is next to the Sea Splash. These tropically hypnotic names tell you the awesome truth—you can walk right out your door to the ocean, pool, and thatched-hut beach bar.

With laid-back inns that stretch to the west toward the cliffs, Seven Mile Beach boasts basket loads of lodging variety, with plenty of hip hotels to choose from. Exceptional high times can be had when choosing to crash along this length of Neptune's rapture, putting you precisely in the center of a geographical chillin' zone. Very *irie*, mon! Handcrafted wood furniture, funky, beautiful island colors, the sweet scent of ripe ackee fruit, thatched huts, hand-painted signs for tonight's reggae beach blast, parrots, pelicans, grilled lobster, people selling everything, Red Stripe by the tanker, ganja floating, people wearing less than nothing and getting burned in sensitive situations—these are all a tiny part of any hotel along Seven Mile Beach. What fun!

The hotels and resorts that line Seven Mile Beach are as varied and colorful as one could imagine, with décor from island plain and simple to tropically cool.

Go online to TripAdvisor to see what they are like and read reviews from other folks who have been recently. This will at least get you started, and you can see a large diversity in prices, but you may save a bazillion dollars staying at a cool place on the beach instead of having your nails done at the AI. Owners, prices, and other things can change rapidly with the seasons, so do your research. To find any of these hotels, just do a Google search, or go right to a major travel site like Expedia, Travelocity, or TripAdvisor.

Here are just a few spots I recommend, but anyplace is good, as you're always close to the fun on the beach, and of course, you're in Jamaica, mon! Your *Chillin'* guide isn't really a hotel thing but we just need to get you headed in the right direction. Don't take our word for it! Read all the reviews you can on every site and make a decision based on what you enjoy!

Remember, the beach is a nonstop, crazy hustle that's warm amusement during the day and a loud, reggae, outer-limit-type party at night. If you want peace and quiet, you better head to the cliffs or that far-away AI.

YELLOW BIRD

www.yellowbird.com

A mellow place with nice grounds is the Yellow Bird, not a party hotel! NO GANJA allowed at the bar. It has a cool beach bar with daily specials, and everyone staying there really seemed to like it. Maybe it's for the forty-five-and-up crowd. It has a nice beach area with security, and I really liked the girl at the bar who couldn't remember my name.

ALFRED'S OCEAN PALACE

www.alfreds.com

Alfred's Ocean Palace is the reggae capital of the beach! (Palace is pushing it.) A plain, old-fashioned party place for sure! Reggae, rum, and Red Stripe, and good local food can be found here. Breakfast and lunch are good and very affordable. You can get a traditional Jamaican breakfast of akee with saltfish, dumplings, and callaloo for about five bucks, and it's very good. Coffee and breakfast on the beach! We love it.

KUYABA NEGRIL

www.kuyaba.com

This place is really cool with great jungle décor, parrots, and lots of bamboo. Rooms look to be a good deal with cheap winter rates. A deluxe room has Mexican tile, French windows and doors, air-conditioning, fans, cable, CD/radio, verandas with hammock chairs, double beds and free Wi-Fi just a few inches from the beach for only $97.00 a night in season. Kubaya has even more rustic rooms or cottages for

$77.00 a night in season. Out of season, it's only $56.00 to stay on the beach—are you kidding?

LEGENDS BEACH RESORT

www.negrilhotels.com

Legends is a nice place on the beach with a bar that fronts the ocean and a little restaurant alongside. The best thing is it's always full of happy party people, and it's always got great rates that include a free shuttle for the short ride between the two hotels (Legends and Samsara) and so you can enjoy both sides of Negril. Rooms are simple but clean, and service is pretty good with tropical landscaping. Always a popular place, it has all-inclusive options so you can eat and drink at both properties. The bar here faces out with a fantastic beach view.

COCO LA PALM

www.cocolapalm.com

This is a beautiful seaside resort that has numerous return guests because of the outstanding grounds, its spacious rooms, and good service. Marley's by the Sea is a very popular restaurant and bar.

MERRILS I, II, AND III

www.merrilsresorts.com

Merrils has three hotels, all about right next to each other, right in the middle of Seven Mile Beach. Nice, two-story buildings with balconies front the sea.

FUN HOLIDAY BEACH RESORT

www.funholidaybeachresort.com

This popular beachside resort has some great all-inclusive rates, with a restaurant serving Jamaican and international eats. They have rentals on the property, and that makes it easy to grab a Jet-Ski, Jeep, or car for exploring the rest of the island. People love this place, and it's lots of fun to hang out in the hot tub here.

CRYSTAL WATERS VILLAS

www.crystalwaters.net

How could anyone not love this place? Really, you could stay here forever. It offers one-, two-, and three-bedroom villas right on the beach, which are very comfortable and have many of the amenities that can make your time here relaxed and easy: full kitchens, air-conditioning, TV, private beach, pool, and Jacuzzi near just about everything. Your own villa is a very private and cool way to blow some time here, and if you're lucky enough to have more than a week or so, the full kitchens will save you a fortune on food. They even have a cook on staff, if you feel lazy.

NEVER SCORE ON THE BEACH

If you walk forever, I'm sure you could drag seven miles out of the beach, but the length of strip that has any action is only a tiny fraction of that. But its name is "Seven Mile Beach," so there. Beaches are always *the* place to hang out. Sand, sea, surf, people of all kinds, all the water sports, parties, hustle, and action are usually along a beach somewhere, and it's no different here. Bars front the ocean like old soldiers waiting for the next round of action, ranging around the front of the beach, ready to do battle with a slew of thirsty heathens. A splendid afternoon can be spent strolling from bar to bar, meeting people, drinking, and falling down in the sand, losing your sandals again. Bars can range from really cool thatched huts with bamboo seats to a picnic table in the sand, and every hotel seems like it has a bar along its beachside.

Every guide with any information about Jamaica is sure to go on and on about the beach hustlers and how to avoid them. Really, it's impossible and way more cool to confront them. Just say "No, mon, respect," or say it like a pro with a quick fist bump and a "'Spect, mon," like you deal with it every day and roll on with the tour. Or take a look at what's for sale, but don't follow anyone selling drugs or ganja who want you to walk up past a shack. NEVER SCORE ON THE BEACH. The local vendors are fun, and if you need some fruit, why not now?

Bargaining is still fun here! Mexico is no fun anymore, because they don't really bargain, or they play with distain. Jamaicans, like Italians, have their bargaining power instilled in the womb. Negotiating can be fun, and they are happy to do it. I'm just saying, you can get to a fair price that's OK with you without any pressure. These guys are pretty good (and relentless) salespeople, but you have the money so don't concede to any sale unless it's one you want to make. Just have fun with it. Buy them a beer, and you'll get a better deal and accidently make some friends. Now, if a Jamaican calls at you from a bar or from up the beach where he is, it's a little different. They will think you very rude to keep on walking and to ignore them. Again, at least respond with a "No, thanks," or a "Respect, mon." Try not to be rude, please, as that can really piss them off, and then some will give you a Jamaican tongue-lashing.

If you ever want to get away from a local, just start walking up to any resort. They all have security, and the hustlers know very well never to travel onto hotel grounds and hassle a tourist. Don't promise them you will buy something if you don't mean it. Say NO. They're used to it!

You are not in a politically correct world here. People say and yell what they want. Young girls alone or in groups might be followed along the beach by young men saying vulgar things that would have them in jail with restraining orders in the United States. Tell them to get the fuck away! No respect! Sometimes you have to show them you won't take that kind of shit from anyone or just turn into any resort grounds and wait for them to go on their way or find any security. The local police have stepped up daytime patrols, with beach cops in white uniforms roaming up and down the water's edge so that's not so likely to happen anymore.

Not all beach vendors are selling ganja, and you want many of the services being offered, such as the fruit and fresh coconut drinks being sold by that nice old lady, or a beachside oil massage, and I always stop the dude with fresh steamed lobsters in a box, and occasional wandering musicians. Rastas mostly sell things they make, and it's amusing to take a look and rap with these folks and buy a few trinkets. The Rastas are not pushy but need to survive, so I almost always buy a little something, and they are really interesting people. Ganja kings!

FAT OLD SUN

What's that burning smell? Most likely it's your skin. If you're not used to this kind of sun exposure, and most folks aren't as you probably just arrived from someplace colder than hell, make sure you go out early in the mornings and in the late afternoons. Doze and play in

the shade during the middle of the day. You will lower your chances of destroying your skin and wasting your vacation under the sheets, slathered in Solarcaine.

Use the hottest part of the day for shopping or hide in a hammock under one of the many generous palm trees that grace this island paradise. If you start burning, retreat to the room with a book, air conditioner, and apply generous amounts of 100 percent aloe vera. (Ganja is also a great pain reliever.) Make an effort to use organic sunscreens only, as most sunscreens have enough bizarre chemical compounds in them to power a bad sci-fi movie. Why smear a toxic cancer experiment filled with chemicals you can't pronounce on your skin? Many organic sunscreens can be found online or at natural food stores in the United States. A slight burn is probably better, and it's nature's way of telling you that you've had enough sun. Don't listen to the bullshit media that tell you sunshine is bad. It's your best, all-natural source for vitamin D. You should get fifteen to twenty minutes of sunshine a day, just for the vitamin D your body needs to stay healthy. Have some aloe around, and don't get drunk in the middle of the afternoon or pass out on the beach. You'll wake up to find someone has swiped your camera and that your skin has begun to resemble the fine pink of a local crustacean on de grill.

YOUR DRIVER

As a visitor to the heavenly sections of Negril, the best thing you can do is find a good driver. It is the perfect connection. A cool driver will take you anyplace, show you chill stuff, and find about anything you want. Most drivers are pretty cool. If you don't like a driver, don't use him. Our last driver took us out for the afternoon, and we bought him some beer and his lunch. You couldn't find a nicer guy, and the four of us had a blast. He came by the hotel the next day to say hi, and to see if we needed anything. We didn't, but we had talked to a nice English couple who wanted to have the same fun we did, so we introduced them, and off they went! You're making friends, and you're helping your driver get more business. What goes around comes around.

Getting a good driver may be the best thing you do! Just make sure you negotiate a price for any trips first! Good, safe service is typical. Most times, your driver will wait for you if you go out, and you can feel pretty secure knowing someone is watching for you. They all have Digicell cell phones, and you can call your driver and he will arrive in mere nanoseconds to pick you up. Always tip your driver, and if you like him, use him all week for a great time. He can easily transport you to the coolest locations in Negril

DEFENSIVE WALKING

When you get brave enough to walk the roads of Negril, every other car will honk at you. It's not your good looks. Everyone would sure like to give you a ride, sell you something, or just get your attention. Try to walk with the traffic, not against it.

Walking on the streets is not for the faint of heart. It takes a while to get used to it, but still, it's a lot of fun, and the people are friendly as you wander away from the seclusion of the beach. Pay close attention to traffic because, as you found out on the way in from the airport, the driving is crazy at best and pure insanity compared to wherever you're from. Along the cliffs, you hug the walls for dear life as motorbikes whiz by, missing you by centimeters, and cars race and dodge each in a traffic ballet of chaos-filled honking madness on the road now called One Love Drive or West End Road.

Norman Manley Boulevard is the main drag or the street that rolls straight behind the beach. It's just a straight shot so you can't really get lost. You don't need a map and walking the road is safe enough during the day.

Soon you'll be renting a bike or motor scooter and will be swiftly zipping around the main drag like a native. Make sure you stick a movie camera or iPhone out the window (not too far out) on the ride home because it's a blast to watch all the craziness on the road as a home movie.

CHAPTER 4
CHILLIN' AT HEDO

HEDONISM II

www.hedonism.com

Talk about twisted! Our choice for the best party hotel hands down for undomesticated nights and possible naked fun is, of course, the illustrious and notorious, all-inclusive Hedonism II, from now on known as Hedo. This palace of the gods has some of the highest return guest rates in the world, and it's the only AI that's any insane fun and one of the *Chillin' Guide*'s top places to visit before you die, or, like they say in Jamaica, "go night-night."

People have been going nuts here forever, with some guests returning from thirty to a hundred times, and loads of fun-lovers go once a year. It's a lot of demented fun, with a super beach area, nude hot tub and pool, water slide, piano bar, swim-up bars, and a crazy, rocking disco with a stripper pole! Various other cool activ-  ities include a spa, gym, water sports, restaurants, gift shop, a small but amusing slot-machine area, and of course, the entertainment staff.

No tipping is permitted, which makes this resort very nice to visit. And really, who can carry money when your firm buns boast no pockets? Fantastic service is the norm, and the staff can be enormous fun. Anyone who has not been to Hedonism has a huge misconception of what it's like, as we did.

Rooms are about the same, but the beach is divided between nude and prude. Great! It's adults only! No little urchins allowed. On the nude side, you should be nude, and on the prude side, be whatever. No photos, please! Hedo is a unique place and welcomes people of all sizes, ages, races, and so on. It's not only for the young, marvelous men and women, although they are everywhere, beautifying the atmosphere. Folks way up in the age bracket love it here as well. Hedo is a freedom thing that quickly becomes an experience, not just a vacation. You'll encounter some fantastic, crazy, party-mad people here from England to Russia and billions of lunatics from the States and Canada. Everyone is so friendly that staying here is enormous fun, and you may observe that people are just happier when naked. No shit, Sherlock.

You're greeted with a "welcome home" at the front desk, and you often see staff and guests hug and kiss, happy to see each other again. It's the Hedo atmosphere. What's really cool is that you become part of a strange, weird, wonderful, happy family. Many of the staff have been here a long time and soon know you by name. Cecil is at the front lobby most of the time, and he will take good care of you, getting you and all your crap to your room. He's a super guy who can help you find anything, go anywhere, or hook you up with a good driver.

If you come in the off-season, the hotel is usually not full, and you have more beach for yourself than you can handle, but the resort can be sold out around Halloween because of the wild-ass costume party. It's also full throughout most of the winter due to the fact it's damn uncomfortable to get naked during a Minnesota blizzard.

Get some coffee and walk down to the beach. There, let your senses soak in the mind-blowing sapphire sea, mixed with the scent of the blooming ackee trees that ring the beach area, resembling an explosion of apple orchards, pelicans freefalling for their food, and parrots in the palms. Wow! It's very chill here, and you'll be trying to dredge up exactly what it was you were doing at four in the morning. If you like to party hard, this is probably the best way to spend a week and one you're likely never to forget. And yes, you'll probably come back. It may be all you think about for a year.

BEACH BALLS

Hedonism has a very pleasant stretch of granular material composed of finely divided particles: sand! You can't help but have a weakness for this wide, long stretch of Bloody Bay, where you can unwind in a painlessly easy manner while gazing at watercraft of all varieties, at water birds running amok, unadorned folks lying around tanning, and large amounts of tropical merrymaking at the nude swim-up bar.

With the paramount length of sand on the prude side, this is also where most of the lounge chairs are located near the shore. You can walk to the nude side, which is just past the boat dock.

Here the beach begins to turn into mostly mangrove trees at the shore, so you have a mix but mostly trees and then an undersized beach that is nude only, with a roped off ocean section for swimming and lying naked with a drink on a raft. It's true that the nude side is insane fun. The resort is not that sizeable, and it's a quick jaunt from one side of the beach to the next, and you'll find it natural to be dropping your drawers in no time. Yes, you will! No one here gives a shit what you look like, so get over it.

Delroy is a cool dude who rakes the beach every morning. Up and down with his long heavy rake, he clears away the night's debris, running long, snakelike paths through the unfeeling shore, long before you've found your first cup of coffee. The view from here is astounding; you look across the bay and can see Seven Mile Beach come to a point while to your right is Booby Cay Island. It's a very nice scene—also very bright with the sun glaring off the diving boats and the sea, blasting your eyeballs. Better not forget the sunglasses.

Even more spectacular, if possible, is the beach here at night. Due to its location on Bloody Bay, far from Seven Mile Beach, the dividing fence and wandering security force help to make this one of the safest beaches at night anywhere. It's totally cool to come down to this stretch twenty-four hours a day, and that is really chilly! You'll never be hassled here. I love this beach at about 12:30 a.m. Before an evening rain, giant clouds will form, and you can catch a glimpse of distant lightning as it makes itself known across that void of mysterious sea. With the ocean breaking and the sound of reggae in the distance, you're the only person on the beach; stand real still and try to absorb these singular moments, then drag yourself back to the disco bar for more thumping, half-naked fun.

4:00 A.M. TO 4:00 A.M.

Any food critic can tell you when food is terrible, with dire effects on one's pallet and stomach, and when it will make you smile with immense satisfaction. You won't get sick from the food here. It's not great local food or five-star dining, but you'll live, and there's enough variety for vegetarians. When your second wind hits, they have a midnight buffet containing lots of greasy fries and cheeseburgers with some other limp munchies that you can't describe—like they know what you've been smoking all day! Your room has a coffee service, but if you can't fumble around with it, there's always coffee and tea in the main dining area. Currently, they have two specialty restaurants, which are included with your stay: Mariano's (which is Italian) and Munasan (which is Japanese). Both are open for evening feasts; both are fun and a good change from the buffet. Truth is, you could provide the guests here crispy fried cardboard for lunch and slightly salty seaweed for supper. No one comes here for the food.

Bars are generous at fulfilling your yearnings, and I can say that Scooter and I have tested that theory to the limit! There is rum in any form and of course, every kind of bizarre, tropical, mixed drink a Parrot Head could long for. The Red Stripe is on tap, and if you hate that, you can buy bottles of Stripe and Heineken from the gift shop. The really good service at all the bars means they seem to take care of you quickly. There's still no tipping, and you won't have to wait for a drink. They do have super bar staff.

There's a main bar in the dining and theater area, a small bar down at the prude pool, a long disco bar, and the crazy piano bar, but the famous little swim-up bar in the nude pool is where all the action is after midnight. Daytime here is mostly getting naked with a drink on a raft hanging out in the sun or propping up the pool edge.

THE INSANE PARTY THAT IS HEDO

This place is whatever you want it to be. I can try to describe it, but you have to live through it to understand it. From the wildest Halloween party you've ever seen to lying by yourself on the beach, Hedo is unlike anywhere else you've ever been.

Its beautiful grounds are filled with pools and a nutty water slide, and the hotel is filled with groups and clubs of different sizes from a few folks to some large enough to take over the whole resort. Make sure you go to the Hedo website and check the events page to see what groups or activities will be going on during your stay. Some may or may not be right for you, and it's always fun to join one. Most have websites with all the information you need to get started. Costume nights and toga parties are very popular, so go online to see what the theme nights are for your vacation and pack a variety of crazy outfits. This is not the place to be shy. Hedo is not a lifestyle or swingers' resort, although if that's what you like, go ahead and join a group. Couples who have been in love or lust seem to have the most fun here. It's hardest for a single guy, as it's not the pickup heaven your mind perceives. But if you like to have fun, you can make it work. It's mostly couples and groups, although single girls here are like golden angels landing on whichever cloud they desire.

A ghost town sees more action than this place in the early dawn; the people who are moving about resemble the local island sea snails in their speed and ferocity. When you do warm up and begin recovering, you can lounge, drink, sun, eat, and lie around stripped, undressed, exposed, unclothed, as bare as the day you rolled out of the womb. Wake up more, and you can kayak, snorkel, sail, Jet-Ski, wind surf, dive, play tennis, Ping-Pong, or beach volleyball. Workout, go to the spa, go shopping, take a tour, and get high under a tree all day. There's stacks of stuff to do! Ha! They even have an adult-activity schedule.

Nighttime is what Hedo legends are made of, and you will experience humans in a feral state of uncontrollable freedom, where being a party animal is not only encouraged, but it's the highest order on the food chain. In addition to the hilarious antics of the entertainment staff, which will have you dying of laughter and trying not to choke on your food, there is a piano bar so strange as to border on psychiatrically disordered. From that happy location, you crawl to the nude hot tub or the disco, which is really a disco with extremely loud, thumping music, a mirror ball, long bar, and stripper pole, which gets lots of use. There, creatures scurry about dressed in costumes and sexual gear of all makes and styles, banging away to the music. No reggae here, just loud disco and grinding dance music, and the party roars until the wee hours of the morn. Write your room number on your arm in marker for easy recall and assistance in case you can't get back there under your own power.

The Hedo gift shop is full of oils, pills, and potions of all types, the same stuff you find in the United States, only twice as expensive (but cheaper than at the airport): sunburn products, aspirin (which is a big seller), Pepto-Bismol, condoms, smokes, T-shirts, sandals, souvenirs, and sexy-wear for the ladies. Two displays will let you know that you're in a party hotel: the rack of next-day-I-feel-like-shit and I'm-burnt-to-hell medicines, and a display of ganja accessories such as glass pipes, papers, and Bob Marley gear. There are a few other trinkets no one can live without, like the little stuffed monkey with dreadlocks. I love the ladies who work here.

Landing at Hedo once should be on everyone's bucket list, unless you are totally hung up, and if so, you need it worse than others. Hedo is out of the ordinary, and I wish somebody had enlightened me about this amusing experience a few epochs ago, so now it's my duty to impart this information to mankind and any other alien life forms out there. Life's short. Go now, before they make a law.

FIVE USELESS TIPS!

1. HAVE THE LOCAL ARTIST WINSTON DESIGN AND PAINT YOUR LOVE ROCK AND THEN LEAVE IT THERE FOR ALL ETERNITY.

2. A SOJOURN AT HEDONISM PUTS YOU A SWIFT KAYAK RIDE AWAY FROM BOOBY CAY ISLAND, AN OUTSTANDING, CHILL LOCATION.

3. HEDONISM DOES NOT GET MUCH HABITUAL BEACH-HUSTLER TRAFFIC, AND THE SECURITY IS EXCELLENT.

4. GET NAKED – IN THE NUDE POOL, NATURALLY.

5. YOU CAN ALWAYS BUY A VISITOR'S NIGHT OR DAY PASS IF YOU'RE STAYING ELSEWHERE.

CHAPTER 5
BLOODY BAY

OUR PAST TIME VILLAS

www.ourpasttimenegril.com

(876) 957-5422

Norman Manley Blvd

Negril PO Box 45

Westmoreland, Jamaica

Monster resorts pick this area of Negril—around Bloody Bay—for a reason; the beach is large and beautiful, with golden-white sand ringed by fruit trees and tropical wildlife. Its relative distance from Seven Mile Beach means there's almost no hustler traffic, and it is a desirable stretch to stay on. I suggest you save a fortune and stay at Our Past Time Villas.

Somehow this little chunk of paradise got away from the big boys on the block; sandwiched right between two large AIs, Our Past Time Villas is a rustic little place that is super clean and so affordable, especially for this gorgeous span of beach. A deluxe room at winter rates is about $120.00 a night, or a regular room is about $70.00. They also have studio/kitchenette rooms from $130.00, so you could save even more and cook your own food, and it still puts you in the exact same neighborhood as those paying $285.00 and $350.00 a night. Their brochure calls Our Past Time Villas a "diamond set in sand," and it's true. Don't expect the Ritz, and you won't want it either.

They have grounds beautifully landscaped by a gardener who cares, and they have a super, quaint little restaurant on the beach, which is the center of attention from about 11:00 till 2:00 in the afternoon, when the Fireman starts his lobster grill going on the beach. Folks flock from the AIs to eat real lobster on the grill and watch

the Fireman do his magic. Are you a rocket scientist? Same beach at less than half the price of other nearby resorts, with a chilly lobster grill and bar? Get the teleportation device ready, Captain!

BOOBY CAY ISLAND

Boononoonos! That's Jamaican for fantastic! Seven Mile Beach is really Long Bay, which comes to Rutland Point, from where it's a quick boat ride to Booby Cay Island, one of the more chillin' places in the world.

Booby Cay Island sits by itself in the ocean, a wonderful home to a multitude of creatures: birds, lizards, land crabs, and even some wildcats. No humans live on the little island, but they have in the past, evidenced by the stairs carved out of stone. There is only a tiny spit of beach, which is where you pull up to be greeted by Mr. Porter as he cooks up a lobster with his wife and son, Kevin, or one of the many fisherman who might be cleaning a morning's catch by a kayak. What a great spot! If you don't kayak, windsurf, or Jet-Ski, you can always

find a snorkel tour that will take you here. Mr. Porter shows up just about every day it's not storming, and he has the lobster grill going on the little beach with Red Stripe and snacks for while you're waiting. Go right out to the trap and pick out a lobster. Then you can wander around or snorkel while it's cooking. Bring twenty dollars for the lobster and about three bucks for a Red Stripe. He always has some cold ones in the cooler. Last time, Ian and I drank them all. This is an amazing place and a time you will never forget. Bring the camera. Snorkel right out from the beach and swim north toward the tip and around the island, watching for light traffic in the pass.

Lots of fantastic sea life surrounds the island: rays, squirrelfish, octopi, large starfish, beautiful fans and corals, plus thousands of conch shells with a hole near the top where they removed the critter. Booby Cay gets its name from the bird that happens to nest here, not the breasts that are so happily displayed around the island. A short kayak ride from Hedo, Booby Cay Island is a very cool place, and it's like taking a side trip to your own deserted island in the middle of the Caribbean.

Booby Cay Island is a place you can chill for an hour or hang all day. It's an island paradise not to be missed. It's very *irie*.

Bloody Bay must have been an unusually gruesome, nasty place back in the day. It got its name from the fact that whalers thought this future vacation spot would be a wonderful place for them to gut every pelagic creature of the sea, and so the water was perpetu-
ally red with whale blood. Aaarrrgghhh, matey.

FIVE USELESS TIPS!

1. WHEN STAYING AT AN ALL-INCLUSIVE PARADISE, DO A TON OF RESEARCH BEFORE YOU GO.

2. GANJA USE IS FROWNED UPON AT MOST ALL-INCLUSIVE RESORTS.

3. BLOODY BAY IS THE QUIETER SIDE OF SEVEN MILE BEACH.

4. BOOBY CAY ISLAND IS CHILLIN'.

5. GRILLED LOBSTER BY THE FIREMAN ON THE BEACH MAKES FOR A PERFECT NIGHT.

CHAPTER 6
THE WEST END IS THE BEST END

ONE LOVE DRIVE

One Love Drive is the new name for the road that takes you away from Seven Mile Beach, past the Negril River where fisherfolk tie up for the night, and through the roundabout and tiny town of Negril. It then leads to the cliff side of the island in a winding, skinny snake of a raceway that loops quickly around the shore, bear-hugging the coast while heading west.

Loaded with cool hotels and funky tropical resorts, roadside stands and bars, friendly people, amazing azure ocean water, mind-blowing, dusk-to-dawn displays of the planet's main star, and some of Jamaica's finest ganja, you'll see why people here say, "The best end is the West End." It is an astonishing part of the island that's not to be missed.

BLUE CAVE CASTLE

www.bluecavecastle.com

The first time you see Blue Cave Castle, you'll probably be on a boat looking toward shore. Then your disbelieving eyes tell you that you're looking at a castle in the Caribbean, and the fact that the castle is made of blue-colored stone will make you do a double take. One of the first really cool places in West End, the Blue Cave Castle rises up from the cliffs in a majestically funky way that finds itself in tune with this ocean paradise of palm trees and the jewel-encrusted cliffside.

Built fifty feet atop an old pirates' cave, the watery tunnels will lead you up to a garden or your room. Large, spacious rooms have numerous carved stone niches and nooks, including the penthouse of the castle. The penthouse, the top of one of the tallest buildings in Negril, also has three large decks on which to sunbathe. The out-of-season penthouse rates start at $120.00 a night.

Booking your room online is easy. The website displays photographs of the rooms and grounds so you can see how cool they are. There's a great restaurant with bar on site, and there's good security with a large wooden gate keeping the property very private. It's another place you have to see to believe.

SAMSARA CLIFF RESORT

www.negrilhotels.com

Carrying on up the crazy drive to West End takes you to the Samsara resort, and its location alone makes it worth the trip. Situated on a rocky prominence, the Samsara is the perfect place to unwind and experience paradise without smashing your bank account into subatomic particles.

Catch your breath and look out the window of your new abode toward an incredible, stunning, aquatic wonder. You've bought the impressive view before your eyes for the price of a room at the Holiday Inn on Interstate 70, only with palm trees and cliffs. No rating system with little stars means anything here. You'll either love it or hate it, and people seem to go both ways. Hanging out here, you are going to interact with lots of islanders and folks looking for a vacation on a budget. It's a bit of a hangout, as the tiny bar has a happy hour in the afternoon, and people float in for the two-for-one special.

Rooms come standard or superior, but the view is to croak over. Just appreciate that your superior-room window will open up to one of the widest views of ocean you may ever have at that price. You are on about the southwestern tip of Jamaica, with its cliff face jutting out from the island.

Superior rooms have oceanfront views, and this is what you should aim for, plus they have ancient AC units that come in handy for fighting the heat and humidity. You can also book the all-inclusive package. Samsara is a good bargain, and it's easy to hang at the bar by the ocean and get plastered with some folks from Brazil without worrying about the tab. If you plan on drinking yourself into an oblivion, you may want to go all-inclusive, and who could blame you? Food on the all-inclusive plan is OK, and you can eat or drink at

either hotel: Samsara or Legends. There's dining in the little café and bar, which have a fair number of outdoor tables that include an amazing view, looking straight out to sea. You won't get excited over the food, but you can live on it well enough, and the service is good. There's a mix of local island sides, combined with some familiar foods like fries and burgers. Certain foods in Jamaica—basically, anything imported—can be expensive, so if you don't feel like mulling around, the AI might be for you. We've done it. Stay here. If you forgot everything, they have a little gift shop next to the bar and a strange little convenience store a half-block away.

Check-in is fast and easy, and the pleasant front desk will accommodate you if they can, but this is not a Holiday Inn. You arrange all your own transportation. Bring everything you'll need short of towels; bring your shampoo, all of it. Don't look around here for free stuff to steal; there is none. If you've forgotten what an ancient TV without a flat screen looks like, come to Samsara where the televisions have buttons and knobs! You can stay in your room and watch it all day if you want, because the price is right!

Grounds here are nice and clean. There's only a small pool and hot tub as the main attraction is the ocean. That being said, the pool is a fun little place to gather, party, and drink away a day.

Ciao, Jamaica, which is an Italian restaurant, is across the street, and next to that is a taxi area. Walking around here is scary because the roads are as narrow as the crack in your ass! Hug the walls and watch out for cars, taxis, and buses on their way to the island's biggest tourist trap up the road: Rick's American Café.

Staying here in a superior room also gets you a free shuttle ride to Samsara's sister property on Seven Mile Beach: the Legends Resort, which is a nice way to discover more of Negril, and it gets you to the beach. The all-inclusive plan also lets you eat, drink, and party at Legends (like the sub-human you are), and that gets you to the reggae beach parties right up on the sand, where you can continue your bizarre transformation.

Samsara rests on a wide expanse of concrete over the fossil reef, with a two-story set of superior rooms. It also has a set of funky single rooms on stilts that face the ocean, and these are super cool to stay in, as your hammock hangs out with nothing but sea in front of you. You are likely to smell ganja in the air. Mmm. Lounges with sail tops are spread out by the water's edge like an assembly of island division flags waving you onward. Walkways and walls lined with flat stone, which is a popular building material here, accent the tropical surroundings. The buildings are low, following the  code that nothing should be taller than a palm tree. The buildings are painted a palette of pastel blues, yellows, and mauves with earth tones. This, mixed with all the vegetation, makes for very pleasant surroundings. The pool may be small and more of a wading pool than anything else, but it fronts the ocean in a spectacular arrangement. It's also very clean. There's no beach, hence no sand gets dragged around everywhere. It's true some folks don't like it. Hotel security is kind of built in. Where the property fronts the road, there's a wall, and there's only one way in and out, with a person by the door at all times. There is no beach, so there are no hustlers, which is another reason many people like the West End cliffs. Right next to Samsara is the ultracool Blue Cave Castle. Activities at Samsara consist of absolutely nothing, except a dive shop that will also rent you snorkel gear. There's no kids' club, no activity directors, no evening plays with lousy theme nights, no ancient musicals, thank God. Chill, lounge in the sun, drink, eat, party. Did you need something else?

Our biggest criticism of this hotel is that there are no in-room safes as of this time, and you have to get a safe-deposit box at the lobby, for which there is a charge of about five bucks. Still, you have to do it, so be aware of that.

CLIFF CAUTIONS

About the West End and its hotels—leave the little ones at home. It's not a good place for children. The cliffs can be very dangerous as there is no smooth entry and your first water is at least twelve to seventeen feet deep at the edge. The cliff face has been eroding for eons and is sharper than…well, you know. Who knows how many people have cut themselves on this rock over the years? Don't be next.

Entry here is not for the faint of heart, and the ladders look older than you. They look rusted to the core from salt. Basically, they're just plain scary. Many people just jump, but you always have to climb out. If you are overweight, not a good swimmer, or have tender skin, you may want to use the beach entrance at as your doorway to ocean wonderlands. Make sure you read the section on sea urchins before climbing around the cliffs and dancing in the waves.

Stand around the cliffs in awe and understand why millions of people have been captivated by this part of the island to the point of near insanity—even to the point of moving here! Past luscious palms and tropical plants, the ocean is five different shades of blue and now it's rippling because the crazy dude in the green and red plywood boat is rolling up to the water's edge, wanting to take you out snorkeling. Great!

XTABI RESORT: MEETING PLACE OF THE GODS

www.xtabi-negril.com

Long before Red Stripe washed the island in its alcoholic splendor, the area around the cliffs was inhabited by the Arawak Indians, who came along and displaced even earlier peoples on the island for the abundantly good living in this part of the world—even without the beer. Thousands of years have gone by, and people traveling to Jamaica can still discover why this part of the island was called the meeting place of the gods by the early Arawak. For breathtaking ocean views and feeling flooding with an extraordinary sense of spiritual connection, it's very hard to beat.

So are the prices! Staying here is a happy, laid-back experience. Xtsabi is truly stunning, with the widely spaced layout of  its superior rooms, which are housed in a number of separate buildings. Across the road, there are very cool octagonal bungalows perched above the cliffs. In total, there are about twenty-four rooms, including six seafront cottages with private sundecks and sea access. These are amazingly chillin' vacation spots. At about $120 a night out of season (April 15–December 15), it is a deal that can't be beat! You'll never want to leave.

Xtabi is a cool place for you to really unplug and leave Babylon behind, by staying in very nice rustic rooms without air-conditioning, TV, or phone! There's only a beautiful rotating fan above your bed, and it's all you need so close to the ocean's cooling breeze. Just let its whirring sound and the chorus of night birds and frogs send you to sleep. It's very basic, so you should bring everything except soap and towels, but the housekeeping is great, and the ladies working there are super sweet. Rooms do have key safes for just a little extra, and you should always get one.

It's only a few short steps across the street to reach the entry to a blue sea, lapping into the caves carved out by thousands of years of ceaseless battering by uncaring waves against the ancient limestone bed of fossils that make up the cliffs. Truly, this is one of the most chillin' spots on the island, if not the world, and only $52.00 a night out of season, and in high season (December 15–April 14), it's only $83.00 for a relaxing night in an unplugged little paradise, away from much of the world's craziness.

XTABI BAR, RESTURANT, CAVES, AND THE REAL GEORGE

Very few places are as chillin' as the Xtabi bar, which hangs over the cliff face and fronts the ocean. No one can adequately describe this vibe. You'll have to show up in person. There's also a super open-air restaurant with great food and service. If you're lucky, you'll have the real George working your table and Kevin at the bar. Then you can enjoy as you stare out at the ocean in blissful wonder and chomp on a conch sandwich or grilled lobster.

The caves used by Arawak Indians, pirates, islanders, moviemakers, bats, and anyone else who loves a good grotto are right below the Xtabi bar and should not be missed. It's very cool to walk around there, with light reflecting off the water into the cave. Look up and notice that it's a mass of ancient fossil fans, corals, and sea life that make up the cliff walls, and try to imagine what kind of time span is involved. Let your head swirl around that for a minute. The caves are very cool.

3 DIVES JERK SHACK

Next to the Xtabi resort hides one of the coolest, chill places to  eat in Negril. It's along the same cliffs and has no frills except a majestic ocean, coupled with mouth-watering grilled jerk chicken, vegetables, fish, and lobster dishes that are so good you could cry.

We've been going here for years, and it's always a highlight of any trip because the combination of raw seaside cliffs, grilled kingfish, red beans and rice, and callaloo can knock off your flip-flops. The 3 Dives opens around two in the afternoon, and your food is always cooked to order on two large outdoor grills in front of the red, green, and yellow shack. The menu is scratched out on a blackboard, and the prices are very reasonable. You can't go wrong here, and this place is high on the chillin' list of places to visit while in Negril.

3 Dives is becoming a bit more known and popular these days, so they have built a little stage, and they now have free music on Tuesday nights, which is starting to liven up the West End a bit. Tour buses are starting to drop loads of people off on their nightly rounds of Negril, and at night, it can get a little crowded so it might be an hour's wait for your food. It's always worth it. Extremely chillin'. They have a fire going out back at night, on the edge of the cliff overlooking the sea, so they have a constant supply of coals for the grill. It just happens to lend itself nicely to the party. Grab another Red Stripe and gape at the sunset with the rest of the happy people.

SEA STAR INN

www.seastarinn.com

Away from the cliffs and beach, there's only one resort that we can say is chillin' for sure, and that's the Sea Star Inn. About five hundred feet away from the cliffs, down Sea Star Lane, in the middle of nowhere, sits this hidden little gem. Grounds are nice with good security. It has spacious rooms, a large pool and swim-up bar, restaurant, custom-built Jacuzzi and a ten-foot waterfall. You'll always find a lot of happy Canadians here, as the owner, Chris, is a native of that fine northern country and was smart enough to move to an island where it's always about eighty-two degrees with a breeze. Accommodations feature large rooms with a dining area and a minifridge, air-conditioning, ceiling fans, TV, and veranda with a hammock. You can have a 450 square-foot room with a king or double bed for only $79.00! Your room rate includes a daily continental breakfast and a beach shuttle. The Sea Star has some very affordable wedding packages that start at around $500.00, so book early, or you'll never get in. And don't forget the One Love Reggae show every Saturday night.

One Love Drive starts to get a little more exclusive as you head farther west, and places can be a bit luxurious with some very high-end resorts along the cliffside. This is a very amazing part of the island, with good restaurants, roadside shops, and bars flung about everywhere. Here are a few of the better-known resorts. As we have no real experience at these fine facilities, please do your own online research to see if they fit your needs and budget.

The Rockhouse Hotel is apparently very nice (www.rockhousehotel.com). Tensing Pen is well-known as a mellow hangout (tensingpen.com). The Moon Dance Cliffs Hotel and Moon Dance Villas are beautiful (www.moondanceresorts.com).

SEVEN USELESS TIPS!

1. THE ROADWAYS ARE CRAZY AND DANGEROUS, SO LOOK OUT!

2. VISIT ONE LITTLE WEST-END STORE, A BLOCK NORTH OF SAMSARA RESORT.

3. WHEN YOU HEAR A LOUD SCREECHING SOUND, IT'S THE GUY PUSHING THE STEAMING HOT PEANUT MACHINE UP THE ROAD. BUY SOME!

4. WATCH THE FLOWERING TREES FOR THE DOCTORBIRD.

5. SNORKELING IS VERY NICE ALONG THE CLIFF'S EDGE.

6. THERE ARE LOTS OF PLACES FOR CLIFF JUMPING.

7. BUY A SOUVENIR FROM DELSIE'S, THE LITTLE SHOP RIGHT NEXT TO THE XTABI RESORT. SHE'LL TREAT YOU RIGHT.

CHAPTER 7
PSSSST, GANJA!

YA MON

YES, I mean yes, ganja is still illegal in Jamaica. It is illegal to have, to smoke, or sell, although it's all over the place. From the airport lounge to the resort gift shop, you can't make a move without seeing a ganja leaf or a picture of Bob Marley toking up. It's a part of the island, like beer, rum, and reggae. If you're looking and would like to add some ultrahappy green island spice to your stay, hang loose, no problems, mon. Anyone can score in Negril, period. It could take you as long as sixty seconds if you're not careful. Hold on to your hats, cowboys and girls. Be patient and hold your horses another hour or so until you pull in at your hotel. Don't get impatient. You waited this long already.

Everyone, well, almost everyone in Negril sells ganja. That's far from the truth, of course, but you will be offered more weed in a week than in your whole life thus far. I have never been to Negril and not been offered various amounts of everything from ganja to hand grenades by a cab driver. People in the marketplace, on the road, everywhere along the beach, any bar, at your resort, and islandwide, all grow or sell a little ganja for some extra dollars to help ends meet.

Roadblocks are common in Jamaica, although it's hard to tell what cops are looking for. They have drastic fines for not wearing a seat belt, and with the maniac drivers in Jamaica, you must empathize with the law because it can only save lives—maybe yours. They also look for drugs and guns. It's probably rare that any tourist bus or transport would get hassled at a roadblock, but anything can happen. It's in your best interest to score at, in, or very close to your resort or hotel, where you are safest from any rip-off. Really, the last thing the cops want to do is hassle a tourist and screw a guest on resort grounds, although it can still happen. Chances are slim you will encounter anything of the sort during your stay, but why take the chance? Pay attention to these common sense ideas and you will have a cool time.

DON'T FLASH YOUR CASH.

NEVER LET ANYONE PUT ANYTHING IN YOUR HAND.

GANJA POSESSION IS AGAINST THE LAW.

Paying too much is a sure sign of an amateur who is about to get nailed! Never pay more than ten or twenty bucks, even for monster, twelve-inch sticky buds! I don't care what they tell you. Act like you like you've been here a hundred times, and when you're going to score, don't carry too much money with you, since almost all the ganja in the area is about the same—that is, it's all good. We have purchased nice, large, fluffy buds for just five bucks. The farther away from the beach you get, the cheaper and better the ganja. Most of the island ganja is really amazing, and sticky buds are wandering around by the bushel. A usual scenario is that someone will whip out a batch of long, natural, on-the-stem, alfresco buds and try to sell them to you at some laughable price, as if you just took a plunge off the turnip truck at night. OK, it's just a test! Some sellers are fishing first in case you bite. Asking how much you can buy for ten bucks usually signals you are not an idiot and tells them they can stop trying to rip you off. Ganja here is not imported but grown right up the hill, probably close to where you're staying. Just say ten or twenty bucks is all you can spend. Tell them you have way more than you need already, (which could be true) and ask how much they'll sell you for ten bucks. If you slow down and rap with them, maybe buy a beer, things will get much better, and you will be quite happy with the purchasing power of a couple of Lincolns. If they get offended, say no problem and move on, as there will be millions of chances and ways to get weed on the island. If you're looking, it will find you. Just don't do any deal you feel uncomfortable about, and remember—Jamaicans can be excellent salespeople.

Never let anyone pressure you into a sale. Never let anyone put anything into your hand. This way you won't spend a lot or get enough to get you in trouble, in case you're one of the really stupid tourists who get caught. Sample a selection of the many varieties that abound by only purchasing small amounts at a time. Buy only green, fresh,  sticky budlings. Don't waste your monkey-money on dried, brown, crispy dead stuff when island ganja is grown fresh all year! Just like when buying produce, refuse anything old or suspicious and purchase fluffy, happy, sticky, green buds on a stem only.

Don't score on the beach or at the nightclubs. Keep it safe and close to your home base of operations. Many folks working around your resort will sell ganja for a little side cash. Gardeners, security guards, cooks, the guys who run the water sports and dive boat, the old lady selling sugarcane and coconuts, bartenders, Rastas, and the girl doing the hair braids—they all sell ganja. Just don't be flashing your cash around, never front any money for any reason, and don't wear loads of bling.

HERBS IS HERBS

Monkey-skunk bud, skunk, herb, ganja, golden Jamaican, sensi, tampi, ishan, indica, weed, rope, good old marijuana, and a trillion (that's a one followed by twelve zeros) other names for the mean green that floats around the island all mean very little when you're buying a big ole bud on a stem that comes wrapped in part of a black garbage bag, or when the lady at the market pulls a six-inch wonder bud from between her boobs—oh yeah. It's all good, with some as sticky and magical as Harry Potter duct tape. If you get lucky, you might hit some real wonder bud, and if you're serious, you could hook up with some Rastafarians, as they are the true believers.

Ganja may be more legal in the United States right now, as Colorado and Washington have just legalized recreational use, and many states have medical marijuana programs. It will come to Jamaica soon! Chronic indoor clone bud is stronger than what you're going to find on the island, but the island ganja is part of the magic, yellow-green puzzle that is Jamaica. Much of the island ganja has a pleasant, mellow high, with an aroma of tropical zing that can't be replicated under grow lights. It's mountain-grown.

FIRST-TIME GANJA VIRGIN

OK, welcome to Negril! You're feeling it, and you're on the beach having so much fun. You've never tried ganja before, and now that you're in Jamaica, mon, you think you'll try a few hits off that monster the locals are passing around or that your buddy just purchased from the hotel gardener. Go easy on yourself, first-timers, because it can still knock you for a loop, and there goes another day of vacation. Island weed is still very potent, and if it's your first time ever, wait until after a light supper. Hang by the ocean blue with a beverage, take about three light tokes, and wait. Relax. Enjoy. This is an excellent way to start, as party time is followed by beddy time.

BE COOL

Lots of people forget this simple rule because of obvious things like beer and spring break—just be cool. Don't go crazy just because someone else is. A Jamaican jail is a hard place for the casual tourist to land, so don't push your luck in a different country. You are subject to Jamaican law while on vacation and GANJA POSSESION AND USE IS AGAINST THE LAW IN JAMAICA. THERE IS NO BAIL FOR TOURISTS! Maybe someone would take a bribe.

Keeping your party at your resort area—in your room or on the balcony—is the best thing you can do. Housekeeping will straighten up your buds if you leave them out in the room.

Still, as many times as you go to Negril, you'll probably never have a problem, and good times are really the blast that passes for normal here. We just want you to have a safe vacation, and don't blame this book for any of the stupid shit you do!

Visit higher regions with a little common sense.

SPACE CAKES AND HAPPY NIGHTS

Space cakes? They sound great! And they are. Want a mellow buzz that quietly works for hours without telltale signs of smoke? Ask any taxi driver where to go for ganja brownies or "space cake." That's island ganja cooked and swirled with a sweet, homemade mix of herbs and brown sugar that will crinkle your brain like an orbital pancake. Yummy. I would tell you here where to go, but let's not print the names. Every taxi driver in Negril knows where to go to get space cakes, and it's all close by, straight up the road to West End. No need for directions. They know to head for a colorful, red and white roadside café, where space cakes are made in the back with loving care. Go on in, or if you feel a little timid doing that, your driver will be in and out in a second. Don't laugh at the cowboy hats and country music. A good-sized brownie is about ten bucks, and so full of ganja that it's more like eating a Star Trek cinnamon roll. If it's your first time with this cupcake-show blue-ribbon winner, go real easy. It takes longer for the full effect to sneak up on you. When it does—kapowee! They pack a punch! Try a quarter of a brownie the first time, and your vacation won't be spent entirely in a parallel universe. Not that it's a bad thing. This is a fine buzz for folks who don't smoke.

DISCAIMER: Don't make this hilarious mistake and eat a whole space cake on the way back to the airport.

Ganja can be made into many things from butter to candy bars, and people tend to be inventive with the holy plant. If you're looking for more information on ganja and what to make with it, you can read up on it in magazines, books, and online. The information is everywhere and easy to find. Many other types of cooked or transformed ganja, such as hash and what's called "finger-hash," are also swimming around the island for sale. If you know what you're doing, and you're in comfortable surroundings, take a look, but some is rip-off material, and no doubt processed through some strange chemical stuff.

My best advice is to beware of these drugs. For ten bucks you get much closer to cloud nine-and-a-half with the space cake, regular ganja, or mushroom tea.

TEDD'S MUSHROOM TEA

Buzz by the roundabout in Negril and continue right past the

Shell station, and you'll find Tedd's Shroom Boom, a favorite place for those wishing to explore even more closely the natural spaces between their ears. Tedd's mushroom tea is cooked to

order, and every batch is made to your selected strength. In fifteen minutes or so, they'll be handing you a little bottle. That is the magic mushroom, ready to drink.

Tedd's is famous as a chilly high destination, and the folks from *High Times* magazine and others have visited and written about the psychedelic wonders of his products. Tedd's place been around for years and years. It even has a menu for your trippy mushroom choice, and a bottle of happy shroom tea starts at just $15.00.

Mushroom tea must be legal or the cops don't care because you couldn't be more obvious, and he's been in business forever. We didn't have the balls to try the mushroom Jell-O shots, but we did drink the lightweight version of regular magic tea and experienced a pleasant buzz lasting about six hours that was very similar to a really trippy space cake and made a perfect addition to an evening's chill.

MUSHROOM TIPS

People from all around Negril sell mushrooms and mushroom tea, and unless you know exactly what you are doing, you should avoid buying raw mushrooms or tea from anyone on the beach or bars. If you want to test your cerebral powers, stick with someone who has been doing this forever. Go to Tedd's. It's very easy to find, and every taxi driver in Negril can be there in minutes! When you buy mushroom products on the beach, you'll have no idea what you're about to drink, or its potency. Good mushroom tea will make the sand turn seven funny Crayola colors.

AVOID ALL HARD DRUGS!

You will be offered everything from cocaine to heroin and many other illegal drugs, such as speed, meth, pills, and countless kinds of unidentified, mystery goo. Don't be tempted to try ANY of these altered drugs for any reason while in Jamaica. Rastafarians won't get near this crap!

Experiencing the Jamaican penal system and putting your personal health at risk trying any of these poisons can really destroy a perfectly good vacation. All hard drugs are illegal in Jamaica, and if you're caught, I hate to explain the kind of pain you will go through. Better hope you have a large bank account back home.

Here are the phone numbers you'll need if you make the mistake of being arrested on vacation while enjoying any mind-altering activity that Jamaican law happens to frown upon.

US Consular Agency in Montego Bay

Whiter Village, Unit EU-1

Montego Bay, St. James

(876) 953-0620

MobayACS@state.gov

US Embassy Kingston

Consular Section

142 Old Hope Road

Kingston, Jamaica

(876) 702-6470

EMERGENCY in JAMAICA is 119.

Airports and cruise-line docks are places that you and your luggage will encounter a complete search, with dogs. Tourists go to jail every year trying to sneak weed and other drugs back onto a cruise boat or plane. Don't try it.

Never carry any package for a stranger.

CHAPTER 7 : PSSSST, GANJA!

LEAVE IT ON THE ISLAND

Take nothing home. Give any leftover ganja, space cake, or pipes with love to your neighbor at the resort. Not one seed goes home, no used pipes, NOTHING. You will go to a Jamaican jail WITHOUT bail! There is no tolerance at the airport or docks. They have dogs and know every trick ever thought of to smuggle drugs off the island. This is just another great way to screw up your trip! Bring nothing home but carvings, beads, and T-shirts.

EIGHT CRAZY TIPS!

1. WATCH OUT! GUYS WILL TRY TO PUT JOINTS IN YOUR HAND ON THE BEACH.

2. DON'T BUY MUSHROOMS OUT OF A SACK.

3. EVERYTHING COMES WRAPPED IN PART OF A BLACK GARBAGE BAG – NO BAGGIES.

4. BUY FRESH, ON-THE-STEM BUDS ONLY.

5. THE BEST GANJA IS ON THE WEST SIDE OF THE ISLAND.

6. DON'T BUY THE CHEAP WOODEN PIPES ALONG THE BEACH. MOST VENDORS HAVE GLASS ONES, AND YOUR THROAT WILL THANK YOU LATER.

7. DON'T BE MR. OBVIOUS JUST BECAUSE IT'S SPRING BREAK.

8. NEVER PAY MORE THAN TEN OR TWENTY BUCKS FOR ANY BUD!

CHAPTER 8
BLOW YOUR MIND ON THE BEACH

REGGAE BEACH PARTIES

Reggae beach parties and shows are everywhere around Negril, and reggae nights are the ultimate island way to trampoozle. Go out and party. There is no reason to waste away every night at the AI searching for the chocolate fountain and watching a pathetic house band playing a Michael Jackson tribute.

When in Jamaica, nothing makes you feel as good as reggae music and a little Red Stripe under the stars, with your toes in the sand. It feels so natural here, an organic vibration rolling around the island, pumping out more soul than Buster Brown has shoes, ya mon.

Read some of the hundreds of colorful signs clogging every vertical object for information on local parties, and you'll see that there's always something going on. Travel in groups of two or more at night if you can. You'll find reggae on the beach mixed with some dancehall and American rock. Caution: you can get stuck in some AIs that play no reggae at all, short of some lame version of "I Shot the Sheriff" in the background. Chilly times and a must while here is a good reggae band wailing away. Ask at the resort or any driver to see if any special shows, events, or guest artists are playing in town, as there are always reggae festivals popping up all over. Here are a few reggae hot spots to hang out at and have an upright musical experience during your stay.

ALFRED'S OCEAN PALACE

www.alfreds.com; (876) 957-4669

Alfred's Ocean Palace, right on Seven Mile Beach, is a great place to go. It's a Negril classic and easy to find, right along Norman Manly Boulevard (the main drag). It's close to everything. They have a nice reggae party three times a week, with two different artists each night, so you can catch a show anytime you find yourself with nothing else to do on a Tuesday, Friday or Sunday night.

It's five bucks to get in, and the show starts at 10:00 p.m. Drinks are reasonable, and service is good. We saw Golda Watson and  Marisko, and it was a lot of fun and good music for a Tuesday night. This is the best thing going on most weeknights, and at times, it can get a little crazy—in a good way—while you dance and drink in the sand. Guys and girls looking for island love can find it here. Just don't go wandering off by yourself. Guys, please realize that many girls here from the island look really hot, and when they come on to you, it may be a business proposition. The sex trade is normal around here, and you will find both sexes working the bars, clubs, beaches, and streets of Negril. You can go here if you're traveling alone. There's security around the bar.

Even when staying close by on Seven Mile Beach, you can't just walk up the beach and get in for free because a magic wall appears in the sand, blocking your entrance. If you want to get in free, go early. Don't bring your ganja. There's no smoking allowed at the beach party! Just outside the door, on the other hand, is a little different.

Alfred's best-kept secret is the food they serve. If you're still crawling around the next day, for about five bucks they have a traditional Jamaican breakfast: salt fish with ackee, callaloo, and dumplings. Try that!

BOURBON BEACH

A few times a week, Bourbon Beach has a wild selection of good reggae shows featuring some great stars, and it's a chillin' experience for real. Guys will be handing out flyers and walking with megaphones on the beach, announcing the latest bands and times. This cool place is a short walk west of Legends along the beach and has one of the best stages and largest dance floors in the sand around. They feature some really fantastically cool reggae talent.

Beer and drinks are reasonable, and a lot of locals come here for the real party. It's a super place to meet people. Prices vary, and they sometimes have an inclusive price that will include all your drinks, and that's a deal! They ring the property by throwing up a bunch of blue tarps, leaving an entrance on the beach. If you're out of money already, just sit  outside and watch the ocean waves roll in, as the moonlight reflects like a light ghost drifting across the sand, and enjoy the vibes. When staying in Negril, put Bourbon Beach very high on your list of chillin' places to party! It's safe and crazy, the way we like it, and located right on Norman Manley Boulevard.

SEA STAR INN

www.seastarinn.com

One of the best times on the island and a must-see is the Saturday night, One Love reggae show and dinner at the Sea Star Inn, which is on the west end of Negril, out among the cliffs area. This show is so cool. The drummers and dancers in this show are not to be missed. The reggae artists that rule here put on an amazing and electric performance. Sasanya, Stephen West, and the Roots vibration band, as well as various guest artists, rock this stage every Saturday night from 7:00 p.m. until around midnight, and we rate it highly!

It's also one of the best deals around Negril, with twenty bucks getting you in for both the fantastic music and the all-you-can-eat buffet, which has a satisfying selection of food from jerk chicken to fried fish and sides from mashed potatoes, salad, rice, and peas to cake and rolls. The food here is very tasty and is part of a very cool evening. Get there early for the two-for-one happy hour from four to six. Really, the Sea Star Drummers are not to be missed. It's one of the best shows in Negril! You will be overwhelmed by these island musicians and the energetic vibe they emit as they bang away on various native percussion instruments.

There's a long bar right by the pool with good service. Chris, the owner, will work the crowd and floorshow, making sure the operation runs smoothly and that you're having a good time. With good service and decent pricing, good food and some of the best reggae music around, you'll see what a bargain it is. Here's the super deal—they'll even send a shuttle and pick you up for free! The free shuttle will pick you up and take you out to the Sea Star Inn for the Saturday evening reggae show. Shuttle times are from 7:30 to 11:30. Call 957-0553 and make reservations for your free pickup. This place is so cool. You can go online at realnegril.com and see the show on a webcam before you go. If I haven't convinced you, that will do it for sure!

Sea Star Road will take you to the Sea Star Inn. The inn is on a side road, only about five hundred yards or so from the West End cliffs. Security at the Sea Star Inn is very good, and the property has a ten-foot fence covered in bougainvillea surrounding the property, adding to the front-gate security, making it a very safe and cool environment if you're traveling alone. You won't get hassled here. There are always plenty of taxis out front, and it's never a problem getting a ride. Either way, it's just a short zip up the road from anywhere in Negril. Highly recommended!

THE JUNGLE

Yes, other forms of music exist here. It's true! Dancehall, disco, rock, and reggae can be found at one of the most packed venues on the island, a place steaming with tourists, spring-breakers, and beautiful people wanting to gyrate on a hot, packed dance floor.

They all know instinctively to make tracks toward the Jungle, Negril's world-famous nightclub. Everyone goes here to party, and some famous people drop in, along with a multitude of guest musicians who frequent the stage.

A younger crowd ready to party hard into the tiny hours of the night is the norm at the Jungle, and you should expect to pay about ten bucks entrance, with Red Stripe and rum as the main staples. Go online, check out some YouTube videos, and see if this place fits your style. It's safe for single travelers, with good front-door security, but as always, just use your head and be aware of your environment.

HEDONISM II

Always fun and still a bargain, considering the crazy times you'll have at this madhouse, the disco at Hedo is not to be missed during your stay in Jamaica. You will almost never hear reggae here, but what you will find is one of the wildest half-naked, thumping disco bars you've ever had the pleasure of stumbling into. Your drinks are included—no tipping! Did we mention it's loud and crazy? It has a long bar and bronze stripper pole, even an official disco mirror ball! It's open every night, with theme parties and extrafun groups always around. Go to the Hedonism website to check on current events and themes before you go and maybe pack a crazy outfit. Hedo's night passes get you into the nearly world-infamous piano bar to hear its almost-music. It's really more of a bar than a performance—a sexy, lounge sing-along party that can have its ultrabizarre space and time moments.

Hedo is very safe and supersecure. You'll never be hassled here, and it's a great place to get island wacky if you're traveling alone. Prices may change, but as of now, a visitor can buy a day or night pass: girls pay $50.00, and men get wacked with a $100.00 penalty for being male. Before you begin crying foul, the pass includes use of all facilities, bars, food, snacks, and the nude pool. Bring a towel and backpack for your clothes. The piano bar, entertainment staff, disco, beach, exercise room, and more, plus the fact that this party is one of the best in the world should put a trip here near the top of your to-do list while in Negril. If you don't have fun here, you are already dead, and nothing can be done for you! Adults only!

CHAPTER 9
ISLAND MUNCHIES GRILLIN AND CHILLIN'

I'M SO HUNGRY, I COULD CHEW MY ARM OFF

There is so much wonderful local food on the island, it's a shame to waste away at the AIs eating pizza, dogs, burgers, fries, and the same bland, fatty foods you find at home. While in Negril, you need to chill on the awesome local foods: jerk chicken, kingfish, callaloo, bammy, lobster, conch, ackee and saltfish, toto, gungu peas, jackfruit, dukunu. An infinite number of unique island foods await your taste buds. Try what you think you'll like. Don't be shy and ask questions. You have nothing to fear from the food itself. Most of it is a healthy mix of seafood, chicken, fruits, and veggies—nice!

Not to be missed is callaloo: a plant that appears to look a lot like spinach when it's cooked and is often used as an extra-yummy side dish.

Roadside stands and folks grilling stuff abound. It's good eating, and the island food of Jamaica is so different that you have to explore. Just kind of wander. You can find lots of good and interesting foods along the stretch of Seven Mile Beach and anywhere along the road. Once you've had some beachside lobster off the grill, steamed callaloo with kingfish, or jerk chicken and Red Stripe, you'll see the light.

Many resorts and hotels have superior restaurants on site and right along the beach they have some fantastic local food. Also, make sure to ask a hotel worker or a taxi driver where the best of whatever you look for is hiding. They always know where the good food is. Here is only a fraction of the cool, chillin' places to eat, in no particular order, but if you're here for a week, try some of these local food havens for sure.

ISLAND ITAL

Vegetarians and vegans love Jamaica for its restaurants and large variety of healthy island eats. Ital cooking is very Rastafarian, having a direct relationship with the earth's organic kingdom—no nasty preservatives allowed. This kind of cooking can make you crazy healthy, and you can eat it forever. Ital means cooked naturally, with organic ingredients, leaving out salt and all the crap the fast-food industries of the world insist on ramming down your throat.

If you happen to be a happy, healthy vegetarian, ask your driver where to go. There are some cool eateries around that are worth your time. Ask your resort or driver to see what's close. There are also lots of places on the beach making healthy smoothies and organic foods. Naturally, the area is full of fruits and vegetables of all kinds. Many a new taste sensation is delicious and waiting to be tried.

There are many books on Jamaican cooking and food at the airport and bookstores, gift stands, and so on. Grab one.

THE SWEET SPOT

Just a tiny little place with a few tables, the Sweet Spot has some of the best eats around! It's located across the street from Alfred's Ocean Palace on the main drag, in a tiny, yellowish building. If you like seafood, order the curry fish with rice. Meals run around $10.00 and are well worth the dough. Locals and visitors go here for regional, off-the-hook goodness. The Sweet Spot is not to be missed for simple, super, delicious dishes.

ROADSIDE FRUITS.

Vendors all across Jamaica and Negril sell fruit of all kinds found growing on the island including oranges, bananas, coconuts, sugarcane, watermelon, and a few you may not recognize. Buying fruit from these stands can be a lot of fun, and it's a great way to keep from starving while saving some money. Buy a bag of sugarcane for a buck or two. It comes in six-inch or longer sticks in a clear plastic bag. Take a bite, chew on it awhile, spit out the pulp, then repeat. Wow. Sometimes a dude will be riding a bike loaded with fruits and will whip out a machete and carve up a cane for you on the spot, very fresh. Vendors will also be selling avocados, bananas, coconuts, and freshly squeezed orange juice along the beach for healthy options and possibly to help balance the alcohol content of your body.

BEACH GRILLIN' AND CHILLIN'.

Loads of fun and happy grills line Seven Mile Beach as people cook up all things in a half-barrel grill to enjoy while you're cruising  the beach: lobster, shrimp, jerk chicken mixed with veggies and rice are all on the menu, with a side of Red Stripe.

For great grilled lobster, find the Fireman in front of Our Past Time Hotel on Bloody Bay. Go to Booby Cay Island or the 3 Dives Jerk Shack and always be on the watch for the dude wandering the beach with fresh steamed lobsters in a box.

ALFRED'S OCEAN PALACE.

At Alfred's Ocean Palace, there's reggae at night and good food on the beach during the day at very reasonable prices. Meanwhile, you're sitting at a little yellow table with the ocean in front of you. The view is worth a million, but your banana-pancake breakfast was only $5.50. It's on Norman Manley Boulevard.

THE HUNGRY LION

This is the best restaurant for Rastafarian organic foods, very *ital*, which means pure or unadulterated, organic, and usually without salt or any bizarre preservatives to weaken your body. Some of the healthiest foods in the world can be found inside these red doors, and you will probably see your first real Rasta here. It's located past Xtabi resort in West End, along One Love Drive, right on the road—a chillin' spot for incredible vegetarian food.

BAMBOO RESTUANT

Roots Bamboo Beach Resort has a nice restaurant-bar combo, like almost every resort along the beach. It's a good place to hang or drink on the fun end of the beach.

KUYABA RESTURANT ON THE BEACH

Kuyaba resort is one of our favorites as far as that cool, island décor goes. This place has so much bamboo, palm, and parrots around the property that you feel like you're always in the thick of a jungle, eating in a thatched hut, and you are! Kuyaba restaurant is set pleasantly back from the beach at just the right distance—close enough to the action but far enough back so that you're not eating sand particles. Large and open, it's a very nice place to stroll up to for a shore lunch on the more amusing stretch of Seven Mile Beach.

XTABI RESTURANT AND BAR

This is casual dining by the cliff edge with a great lunch menu. It's rarely crowded during the day and has another amazing view of the ocean.

3 DIVES JERK SHACK

This place is always good and super-casual. You'll be wandering about the cliffs with a beer as they grill your food. They have free music on Tuesday nights, and it's an easy walk from the Xtabi resort. This is the only place you *have* to go to while in Negril.

TEDD'S MUSHROOM TEA HOUSE

OK, we didn't try it, but he's supposed to make a mean and trippy mushroom omelet! It's a half mile from the roundabout, past the Shell station. Any driver can find it.

DELSIE'S PUMPKIN SOUP

It's very easy to make friends while in Jamaica, and you should try to make a point of getting away from the hotel and talking to the regular folks who are working, selling crafts, and fishing, and so on.

Delsie sells crafts and some clothes out of her shop, which is just west of the Xtabi resort. We just started talking and within a few…

pumpkin soup, wow! If you really want to try good food while in Negril, make a friend. You'll be glad you did. Delsie is a kind soul and is indicative  of why so many people love the people of this island. If you are ever staying by the cliffs, or if you go to 3 Dives for jerk chicken, go across the street and say hi to Delsie.

STAYING WELL

Food adventures are easy and fun. You don't have to go far or travel to the outback to sample some out-of-this-world Jamaican food. One thing about the food here, as with lots of islands, is that it relies heavily on fruits, vegetables, seafood, chicken, and goat—which sounds like it's a very healthy diet. Most of the local food is grown on the island or comes right out of the ocean blue, and the chickens aren't bred by the millions, crammed in factory farms, eating bio-injected feed, and the goats run wild during the day, foraging on the tall grasses and assorted jungle stuff. A massive amount of fruits and veggies of astounding variety are grown on the island. There's probably fruit growing all around your resort, like the ackee tree. It's the one that looks like an exploding apple with black little seeds inside. It's the national fruit, and they put it on everything. When the ackee fruit opens, they knock them down, toss the seeds and skin, and keep the fleshy white stuff for cooking.

Here are a few ideas about eating around Negril while still keeping yourself from ending up sick, curled into a ball, watching reruns on squeaky cable in your room while everyone else is playing in the sand.

Getting gut-sick on vacation from junky food- or waterborne bacteria eating away at your stomach lining is about the worst thing that can happen during a trip. Our digestive systems, not used to the upset in the food chain, can react rather violently when attacked by some strange, unsanitary bug, forcing you to spend time on the hotel ceramic throne. Taking some precautions to ensure good vacation health should be mandatory anytime you leave the United States and go to the southern hemisphere. On the other hand, I have never gotten sick from food in Jamaica, and you are much more likely to catch a stomach bug in Mexico.

Use bottled water for freakin' everything if you are prone to getting sick easily or have stomach problems already. Use it for drinking, brushing your teeth, washing your face, cleaning any fruit or veggies you have, or anything else uncooked. You should pony up the cash for bottled water, and it's free at many all-inclusive resorts. When you shower, keep your eyes closed and mouth shut, and try not to get any in your waterways. Pesky bacterial critters don't seem to live in the water system here, but you can't take any chance with your health, as bad drinking water can really mess you up. Stick with bottled water, even in the nice resorts and even more so in the cheap seats. That said, Jamaica has some of the cleanest water in the Caribbean, and you will probably never get sick. Many cruise ships will only take on water here.

One thing you can do before going off to strange environs to keep your stomach in one place is to start taking our friend, the pink one, yes, the mighty Pepto-Bismol tablet. Buy them by the pack; eat them by the handful! What you really need to do is, a week before you go, start chewing one Pepto tablet a day. Have one a day while on vacation and one a day when you return. Hmm. Three weeks of Pepto…that's twenty or so tabs a person at least, plus more in case you get sick. Purchase some acidophilus pills also and take one every day you're there, as they will help with digestive enzymes. If you already have some form of intestinal damage, ignore all this and eat only prepackaged food from the

States and the most horrible, bland-tasting, overcooked food from your resort.

You should also consider bringing along Cipro, or ciprofloxacin. It is a very strong antibiotic, and in the States, you'll need a prescription to get it. Tell your doc you're going out of the country and that you would like to be proactive about your health. Ask if Cipro is something you can take. It has a reputation for attacking strange island pathogens that are hard to find but make you sick as a dog. We never travel without it.

If you get really sick or hurt for any reason, seek medical attention pronto. Most large resorts have a nurse or medical staff right close. If not, find someone to help you ASAP.

CHAPTER 10
SEX WAVES

STRIP CLUBS

Very simple, guys: avoid the island strip clubs. Wait until you get home. Strip clubs have been known to trap unsuspecting visitors inside and lock the doors, then proceed with any number of dangerous rip-offs and a variety of ways to get your cash. Things can become scary very quickly. There are two strip clubs in Negril: the Triple X, which is a single room and a pole, and the Rub-a-Dub, a place so scary we won't get near the door, and we have balls of steel, so forget any review. If you're crazy enough to go, make sure you're in a group of four or five with at least one large-ass guy! It would be better to save your money, and you'll have a way better time at any club in the States. If you must see naked people dancing, you would be far better off purchasing a Hedo night pass. Believe us when we say the strip clubs are not tourist friendly—scary is a better word. AVOID the strip clubs no matter what any taxi driver tells you. If you want trouble, this is how you find it.

AN ISLAND SEX WAVE

Jamaicans are absolutely some of the most beautiful people in the world. Some magic on this island can't be explained, and when you see a local god of either sex, you'll understand. Try not to hold your breath or stare too long. Yo eyeballs is poppin' out. Now, take these beautiful but poor people, trapped on the island without work, just trying to survive any way they can and mix them with (relatively) rich people on vacation who are horny and high, and you can see how this all starts.

Negril has a booming sex trade, and you may find males and females on the island to be quite aggressive in their approach. Prepare to be grabbed or groped if you're alone or if you look like you're looking. Men and women have come to this crazy island paradise for local interactions and love since time began, and many great relationships are formed here. Not everyone is for sale, but as a tourist for a week or so, you may start to think that's the case. Millions of real relationships are formed by Americans, Canadians, Europeans, and Jamaican people all the time, but that's a different story.

Girls have been arriving in Jamaica from Europe, Canada, and the United States by the plane- and boatload forever, looking for love, even if just for a short while. Many women take care of their own special Jamaican man year after year. They used to be called Rent-a-Rastas, and their girls bring them gifts: new shoes, cell phones, cash, and love. They are well taken care of and have a special status. Ask any Jamaican man, and he will expound upon that most important element of male national pride: the native wood.

Jamaican men have a variety of sexual stimulants that they drink like soda pop. They're called "boosters" and they're sold at almost all the bars in little, hot-sauce-sized bottles. Might as well try some before your mate gets a wandering eye.

SEX, HIV, AND AIDS – ADVICE FOR DUDES

HIV on the island is common—and dangerous. Keeping things in your pants until you get back home is good advice, but surely, we are not preachers! Follow these common-sense rules if looking for SEX and love with these wild island girls.

GUYS! Caution rules here, and unprotected sex is a very bad idea. Because of the poverty and other social issues too deep for a travel guide, girls are for sale everywhere, and many men take full advantage of that situation. If this is your plan, make sure you bring the highest quality condoms from home for your protection. Island condoms are cheap, and you don't want to take a chance at catching anything. Also, condoms around the world are different sizes: smaller in Asia and bigger in Africa. Make sure you bring a quality condom that fits you. Almost all the working girls carry condoms with them, but it I wouldn't trust those brands for a split-second. It will be a lot safer to bring quality rubbers from home. Use a condom for everything, even blow jobs, or you can be putting yourself in line for any number of unhappy, communicable diseases, which is another great way to screw up a vacation.

HOW MUCH IS THAT PUPPY IN THE WINDOW?

Local guys all over the island will know where to find girls, just in case you haven't already been approached a hundred or so times. Girls are the next item in line for sale, after ganja and wood carvings. Again, avoid taxi drivers and let someone at your resort hook you up. Where you are, how you look, whether you speak the lingo, whether you're looking, and a million other variables will determine how many greenbacks you end up shelling out. Most girls work for themselves and might give a cut to their referral. They usually don't work with pimps or gangs like in the States, but they are still only in it for the money. If you think any differently, these pros will nail your wallet to the wall. If you can't tell a working girl from someone just being friendly, I can't help you now, but think about it. When you're out at night, is there any other real reason a hot local girl would be messing with you? You don't think you look that good, do you?

I can't tell you what to pay, but like everything else on the island, the price will start high and should end low! While you're wasting money on her drinks, you better be negotiating a price, because she thinks three hundred and you think fifty and you will get to fifty or a hundred bucks. Hang on. It will work out. Please remember these girls are the world's second- or third-best hustlers, behind only Italians and maybe Egyptians. It takes balls and a good sense of humor to bargain with any of these people. If they pretend to be insulted and try to drag more money out of you, just tell them it's no problem, no big deal—like you bang island girls all day back home—and that you might move on. This usually works. Many times, the girls are more reasonable and getting to a price is easy. It always depends on the girl and the place. You'll figure it out.

Finding girls is easy here, but it's just as easy to lose your head, get taken to a dark corner for a blow job, and have a knife pulled on you when your pants are down—another great way to screw up your night.

Find a girl through a local at your resort or hotel—better safe than sorry. Some resorts have a no-working-girl policy, and at others, you will need to sign her in as your guest. Most places, you go right to your room, or they will drag you to a shack, palm tree, or the back of a taxi. The main goal for a working girl is to find a sugar daddy on vacation who will check them in at the resort for a wild week of lust and love. I see men with multiple partners all around Negril, and it's not unusual to have a couple girls stay for the night or week. Some girls live in such poverty that a hotel room is the ultimate in luxurious living: TV, hot showers, and food, with the promise of money for sex and living without struggling for a while. Have your driver zip you around the side streets of Negril if you want to see how hard the living here can be. Don't be cheap, even if you just buy a local girl some drinks. Not everyone lives in such poor conditions here, and there are many amazing estates and beautiful homes in Jamaica, but that's not where these girls come from.

Who knows? You might find love and end up like lots of men, with a girl for the duration of your stay. Then you can come back year after year to a little island love nest. You wouldn't be the first bitten by the island-vampire of love. Please don't promise these girls you will bring them to the States or marry them, unless you really mean it!

THE CHECKUP

Bars along the beach, the beach itself, clubs, and behind the palm trees are all places that the girls will find you. Like ganja, you don't have to go looking. They will find you very quickly. Try to be very cautious with your hygiene and what girls you choose. It may be night. You may be drunk and high at a club or wandering around the beach. Those are the perfect conditions for making any number of colossal mistakes. Examine any girl you're talking to for the following symptoms: way too much makeup, unnaturally yellow eyes, skinny past the point of a beanpole, and bad teeth. None of these are good signs, especially bad teeth. Most healthy Jamaicans have a bright, super set of choppers and are famous for that smile. There are healthy girls on the island, and many carry papers—doctor's reports showing they've been checked out for HIV, STDs, and assorted sexual bugs. Listen to Yoda and choose wisely.

LOVE AND LUST FOR BIG GIRLS

Girls and women from all over the world travel to Negril looking for love or lust, hunting for native wood in groups, gangs, and singles. Jamaican men love white girls and vice versa. A bartender friend often cries on about how he only wants white women, and how he misses working on the beach where he got to meet so many more than he does at his current location. These guys are so charming and handsome that it's very hard for a girl to resist them. They are persistent, the ultimate schmoozers, and they are very good at what they do, as evidenced by the number of happy women in the area.

Copious amounts of sexual energy waft through the air like a hot, swirling sandstorm. This island's all about the love, in case you didn't know. A great destination for single girls and groups of women of all ages is Hedo II (see the list of hotels). You won't be driven nuts here, and you can be anything from mild to wild. Stay for your whole trip or purchase a day or night pass. Hedo is a place where you can be worshiped like the queen you are, or left alone to get naked with a Dirty Banana on a raft, floating around with your butt gleaming in the sun, while dipping your hand in the gentle blue sea as a slight ocean breeze curls your hair. You can drink and party like the insane wild girl who's hiding inside without worrying that you'll  be the next YouTube sensation, as there are no cameras without permission, and no photos at all on the nude side. Security will take your camera and ask you to leave if you're caught taking pictures.

Girls love this place. Go online and do some research. Everyone is welcome: all shapes, sizes, ages, races, and creeds.

CHAPTER 10: SEX WAVES

YA SUH NICE!

All girls will find the love or lust they are looking for here, whether it's a one-night stand or a lifetime. Just use common sense and caution. Stay in groups if you go out wandering. Use a good driver who will stick with you and wait for you until you are done partying at a club or bar. Get to know a driver who will watch out for you—many will, and it's nice to know you'll have a ride waiting for you.

Single girls on the island appear to get the goddess treatment anywhere they go, and there are tons of good-looking Jamaican men to choose from, with strong white teeth and rippling black back muscles. Don't expect lots of romance or dining out unless you're buying. It's part of the gig. You don't pay them, but you purchase everything. So spend it.

Jamaican men do not like to cover their manly parts. It's up to you to insist they do. Yes, it can be like covering a rose in plastic but better safe than sorry. Trust me. These dudes get around, so make sure you bring high quality "boots" from home if you plan on sampling the native hardwoods.

PERSONAL SAFTEY FOR GIRLS!

You may also want to be left alone on the beach during the day, and some of these guys can be relentless. Good luck. You may have to find security. All the beach resorts have security. If anyone starts giving you a hard time, just tell him to bug off or head up closer to any hotel or resort during the day, and you won't be followed. If you want nothing to do with Jamaican men, and you're here alone, or even with a group of girls, pay attention to this easy advice.

Use more common sense and keep the danger radar up more than at home. Never put yourself in a strange or compromising position. Learn to say NO! Don't just go anywhere with some guy who says he wants to show you a special part of the island. Use legal JUTA taxis only. Red license plates, remember? Don't go driving around with local men. Don't leave the beach alone. Don't wear beach attire on the street or while shopping. Don't get a Jamaican man to second base and decide you want to stop. It's rape waiting to happen, and it's a terrible fact that rape is a common practice on the island with little law enforcement or cops that care because you're in a very male-dominated country. Don't expect the police to react like they would in your home country. Sexual assault can and has happened at resorts, so be aware at all times. Use your head and keep the party at your hotel or on the resort grounds. There are tons of single guys from the United States, Canada, Europe, and around the world playing here, so you crazy women have many choices while in Negril. Be smart, have fun, take pictures.

YIKES! SIX USEFUL TIPS

1. DON'T CARRY OR FLASH A LARGE COIL. THAT'S A WAD OF CASH TO YOU.

2. DON'T EXCEPT MIXED DRINKS FROM STRANGERS. DATE-RAPE DRUGS HAVE BEEN USED ON BOTH SEXES.

3. DON'T GO ANYWHERE STRANGE FOR SEX. STAY AROUND YOUR RESORT.

4. DON'T GET SO BLASTED THAT SOMEONE COULD TAKE ADVANTAGE OF YOU WITHOUT PERMISSION.

5. USE PROTECTION FOR WHATEVER YOU DO! ALL THE TIME!

6. STAY TOGETHER AND WATCH YOUR BACKS.

HUSTLERS.

Island hustlers abound by the millions. It seems everyone is in direct competition for that green piece of paper that they hope you're willing to fork over. Tips are expected at every turn, and most people aren't very shy about asking. It makes some folks insane, and really, it's about how you handle it. This is one reason why a no-tip resort such as Hedonism is popular.

Some people hate Jamaica and will never return because of this attitude and the inescapable, abounding, endemic poverty on the island that is always in your face. You just have to deal with it. If you want a vacation in a quaint village by the sea filled with boutique shopping, folks fishing in yellow hats, people riding bikes and waving hello, you need to turn around and head to Duck, North Carolina, because you're in the wrong place.

I hope you know how to shake your head or look at someone incredulously and say, "No, mon. What are you talking about?" or "I got no money to spare," or "Respect, mon. I'm tapped out," or some words to that effect. Then you let it roll off your back and get on with the tour. You might be accosted by a variety of folks all missing body parts, begging on the beach, and you will notice that there is no real health-care system or much government assistance here and it's hard to deal with these sights and conditions the first time here if you're from the States because we have common access to medical care. You will notice that Americans are spoiled to the max, so when you return home, you'll doubly appreciate how rich you really are. I will almost bet that the poorest person you know has a microwave oven. I always give money away when I see a guy with one leg who's got a stick for a cane. Give some cash away. You just can't do it all the time.

TIPS.

Now, the people you do tip are the ones that help you, and if you tip well, you will be richly rewarded by great service. This is not the time to be a tight-ass. The locals work hard, and most have a standard of living that would curl your naturally straight hair, so helping them out with some extra vacation bucks is the best thing you can do for the people and economy of the island. Carry some small bills with you for tipping, and don't flash your cash around in public. Don't bother exchanging money for the short time you'll probably be here, and let them make eight cents or so on a dollar. They'd rather have the greenbacks at this time, and they will love you for Euros. Bring lots of ones, fives, and tens for spending. Avoid larger bills, as there is always trouble with correct change.

CHAPTER 11
CRIME AND COMMON SENSE

IT'S A CRAZY WORLD

It's a fact. As a tourist on an island, you're trapped for a week or so, and the people working the island hustle know it. If you don't live here, you stand out like a broken traffic signal. It's OK. They're just trying to earn a living—and it's just done a little differently here. So here's rule one: NEVER let anyone put anything in your hand, or around your neck without your permission. Someone will try to put ganja or some trinket in your hands sooner or later. Say, "No, thanks. Respect," and go on with your tour.

Local islanders and most Jamaicans are a lot of fun, and you can't help but to hang with them. Some can be great, while others are very weird. If you're not used to it around here, don't go on a walkabout alone, although daytime is pretty safe in Negril's tourist areas. Go with as many people as you can if you stray off your resort, especially if you cruise the bars or beach at night. Seven Mile Beach is safe enough during the day.

Crime is a dirty word in the tourist industry, and no one wants to talk about it. You don't have much to worry about in the Negril resort area, except random theft and just being stupid. Most hotels and all the all-inclusive resorts have tons of security guards wandering around, with mean-looking pictures of guard dogs on their jackets. Make sure you keep anything worth more than twenty bucks locked up in the room safe, including (and most importantly) your passport. Before you leave, look online for some modern anti-theft products to keep pickpockets at bay. Many cool products are to be found, from underwear with hidden crotch pockets for bills, to modern wallets with chain locks.

Crime is a huge problem in Jamaica, much of it centered in the Kingston area and south. Do not go to Kingston! Unfortunately, where there's money, people, drugs, and so on, there's always someone waiting to ruin your day for some dough. Use your head. Get a hotel with a room safe, and no flashing wads of cash in public or wearing every ounce of bling. Don't leave any article

CHAPTER 11: CRIME AND COMMON SENSE

unguarded, no matter where you are in the resort or hotel, and never leave your beach bag out of reach.

Most crime here is theft and common give-me-the-money-first scams, but crime appears to be getting worse everywhere around the world, and Jamaica is having a lot of problems with crime, guns, and poverty. Still, Negril and the areas away from major cities are much safer. Just don't make yourself a target, which is another reason to score only at your hotel. Jamaica is known for its high crime rate compared to other Caribbean islands, but if you're from Chicago, the crime in Negril is for kids, baby stuff. A year's worth of crime might match up to maybe five days in Chi-town, and that's from the 2011 statistics: a murder rate of about nine people, and sixteen break-ins or so. It's getting worse. On October 13, 2012, in the Windy City, two teens were killed, and twenty-four others wounded; and the 2013 crime stats are off the chart.

Try to put your unsuspecting self in the strange position many island people are in, and you can understand (and therefore deal with) their actions a little more easily. Many people are very poor or work for low wages, and everything is expensive if it's imported. They see you on the island and assume that if you can fly, you must be rich, and they sure could use some of those dollars. Many Jamaicans still live in conditions that would freak you right out, and some are in desperate situations, so you must use extreme caution in certain areas of the island. Yet, as many times as I've been here, I've only had to deal with a few crazy people, just like at home.

Some real crazies are wandering around because of the very poor health-care system, and others appear so high that the word *stratospheric* comes to mind. It's best to avoid the ones mumbling and drooling. Use your head, and everything will be "cook and curry." That's Jamaican for A-OK!

US and Canadian government websites issue travel warnings and advisories for countries around the world, and you should look up any country you're visiting before you leave and pay attention to current warnings and conditions.

TEN USEFUL TIPS!

1. LEAVE THE GOOD JEWELRY AT HOME.

2. NEVER LET YOUR CAMERA OUT OF YOUR SIGHT.

3. CARRY SMALL BILLS.

4. TRY NOT TO WANDER OFF THE BEACH WITH STRANGERS.

5. DON'T TAKE MIXED DRINKS FROM STRANGERS.

6. AVOID ALL HARD DRUGS AND DEALERS.

7. STAY IN GROUPS WHEN YOU CAN.

8. THE BEACH CAN GET SCARY AT NIGHT AWAY FROM THE RESORTS.

9. NEVER FRONT ANYONE ANY MONEY.

10. JUST BE COOL. USE YOUR HEAD.

CHAPTER 12
NATURE BOUND

FARTHER ALONG THE ROAD

When taking any excursion in Jamaica, make sure your driver has a late-model car or van. If you negotiate a better price for a trip with someone who is driving a moving junkyard, your sore ass will regret the ride the moment you roll onto any Jamaican back road—and except for the main road, they're all back roads! For any day trips away from Negril, it's best to use a better-known tour operation, private service, or a driver you've had a good experience with. Jamaican back roads have numerous holes the size of moon craters and navigating the twisting, turning mountain lanes during the usual, unexpected tropical storm is not much fun in a broken-down van with a flat tire.

Jamaica is blessed with astounding wildlife: all forms of incredible flora and fauna, hummingbirds in stunning variety and diversity, water birds and parrots, color-changing lizards, monstrous land crabs, crocodiles, fish, shellfish and sea life of all kinds, majestic coconut palms, gorgeous streams, rivers and waterfalls graced by millions  of butterflies, bats and bees that adorn the wilder side of Negril. Pay attention to what's flying around you.

BEACH HORSES

A fantasy that can come true easily enough is riding a horse along Seven Mile Beach in about a half a foot of water, just on the edge of the surf, galloping along at a slow clip under the sun. What could be better? While you're hanging out on the beach, sooner or later someone will ride by on a horse and ask you if you want a ride. Great fun!

ACKEE TREES AND HUMMINGBIRDS

Ackee looks like a small, red apple tree, where the little red apple pops open to reveal three medium-sized black grapeshot-looking dark black seeds. They're hard to miss, and ackee trees are everywhere in Negril and across Jamaica. If there's a season, you wouldn't know. It seems like the stout little trees are always open, or in all stages of opening. Don't eat the black seeds. They're for the birds. Humans eat the mushy stuff on the inside.

Sit under one of these green and red explosions of fruit and watch the wildlife, sip your beer, and listen to the ocean's soft swell. Maybe a yellow-billed parrot, *Amazona collaria*, will land above you. These parrots are not very big, a little more than six inches, and they're endangered and live only on the island—another great reason to lie around high under some trees!

Jamaica's national bird is the doctorbird, which is maybe one of the world's most beautiful hummingbirds, and you'll get the chance to see one. With its long swooping swallowtail-type feathers, it's a real beauty to observe. Hang around flowering trees and wait for them to show up. Negril is always in a constant state of bloom, with flowering trees and plants everywhere. It's one of nature's most mystical landscapes. If you are a lover of all things natural and avian, don't neglect to carry along a tiny modern binocular. You'll have a good chance to see these and many other indigenous species while in Negril, as you're in an area where the great morass, jungle, mountains, and the ocean all come together, providing a happy place for birds and other wildlife to thrive.

CHAPTER 13
WATTA

WATER

The wet and wonderful waters that bless Negril can vary from the seaside, ocean cliffs, sandy beach, and wild waterfalls, to jungle rivers

and streams. Imagine yourself swimming in a breathtaking, blue-green bath of parrotfish and lettuce coral, the ocean so translucent that you can view large cushion sea stars flat on the bottom, stingrays gliding around having fun, needlefish bounding away from predators, and many other incredible sights. With each trip, there's a completely new and different scene to experience. Very irie, mon. Since the ocean reefs around Negril are protected, they are usually clear with good visibility.

Snorkeling can be very liberating, as there's no need to be dragging tanks, hoses, assorted gauges, and gear with you. Snorkeling allows you to range around the shallow reef areas and caverns, exploring colorful and mysterious sea life without being scuba certified. Snorkeling around Seven Mile Beach is great, and some spots are fantastic. It's safe enough if you're a decent swimmer.

Wait around for a local dude to show up in a red and green plywood boat, offering rides to the reefs. These trips range from an all-day party with lunch and beer, to a few hours of cruising some shallows, or whatever you feel like doing. Fix the price before you go, and if you have a good time…tip your boatman. Our glass-bottom boat had an old picture window fitted into the bottom covered with a plywood sheet. It worked. When lodging around Seven Mile Beach, ask for our good friend Captain Jack. He can drag you out to Booby Cay for a grilled lobster on the island or take you to any of the little reefs and cliffs in the area for a good snorkel. He has one of the nicer motorboats tied right on the beach. Ask around for him. He's a lot of fun to go out with, and you'll have a cool time for sure!

Grab a color guide to the local marine life so you know what you're looking at. It helps. Don't touch any kind of coral; many corals are very sharp and will rip you a new one. Also, things like fire coral are everywhere in the ocean and will burn you like a cigarette pushed into your skin. Avoid lionfish and anything that looks like it might be called a fireworm. Do amaze your buddies by pointing out that the living turd they just picked up is a Donkey Dung sea cucumber. Don't go lifting rocks or dead coral on the bottom looking for sea creatures. I did this a lot until, while diving off a beach in Curacao, I was bitten by a moray eel hiding under a plate. You can always snorkel right out from your hotel. Ask around for the best spots near shore. Just offshore from the Breezes resort you can see a cannon and anchor in about six feet of water.

The water off West End is fantastic for swimming and snorkeling, and people cliff jump all up and down the coast. Lying around on one of many cliff faces that border the ocean, it's easy to slip into the blue-green water to snorkel around the sides and caverns while looking at a wide variety of aquatic life through crystal clear water. Cliffs all around Negril are very fun to jump off of, but use extreme caution if you don't want to end up cut to ribbons by the extremely sharp rocks and coral that ring the sea's edge. People get hurt and even killed doing stupid stuff every year around the world, so please don't get drunk and go cliff jumping! It's a bad combination that only sounds like fun.

The area of Negril called West End starts (more or less) just past the roundabout. There you'll find lots of very small resorts and places to eat. The area around the cliffs is a favorite part of Negril. Don't miss a snorkel trip to West End. Ask your driver! If you stay at one of the small resorts along the cliffs, they'll have to drag you away kicking and screaming at the end of the week.

WATER GODS

The stunningly beautiful waters that grace this slice of Jamaica are everywhere to be explored, swum through, fished in, and played upon. Waterfalls, jungle rivers, springs, the Caribbean Sea, and our favorite—the unexpected tropical rainstorm, are all part of the island's mysterious and fantastic watery pulse. Veins of rivers and waterfalls snake and flow through the great morass of swamp and jungle as the water heads out to its new home, the sea. Along the way, it feeds and replenishes life on the island. Grow, little ganja! Grow!

Jamaica can get everything from an all-day drizzle to a full-blown hurricane, but much of the year it's between seventy-nine and eighty-five degrees with a slight breeze blowing in from the ocean. Yes! Ocean water in Negril is always warm enough to play in, anytime you go. Throughout much of the year, you get an afternoon rain and then the magical, tropical clear up. The sun comes back out, and the lizards scamper around looking for supper and crabs hunt tidal scraps while you consume another Red Stripe and contemplate your next adventure.

LONG-SPINE URCHINS.

All around Negril in Jamaican waters lives the happy *echinoderm* known as the long-spine urchin, or sea urchin—or, to the person who just stepped on one, the black spiky thing from hell. They slowly walk around, eating slimy algae off the sea bottom and generally seeming to enjoy life, as they have for millions of years. If you are unlucky enough to step on one or grab it, the thin spines snap off and work themselves deep into the surface of your skin. They are far worse and harder to remove than a splinter, and you will scream and cry for mercy trying to get them out. These can become infected, and you may want to seek medical assistance. Use water shoes when waking around in shallows and cliff areas. Many places in the ocean are thick with urchins, and it looks like a carpet of black spikes waiting to attack you. A way of softening up the skin is to use some acetone and then dig. Remedies are brutal. Do not pee on a jellyfish sting! Pick off the tentacles and wash with vinegar, or seek medical attention.

LAND CRABS

Large blue-and-grayish land crabs, some with shells the size of a Subway sandwich, live happily at many fine resorts on the island. If you're on Seven Mile Beach, there's a wonderful chance one of these crustaceans will cross your path at night as they rustle  around, looking for scraps, and you're stumbling around, looking for drinks. Don't freak unless you have a severe case of *ostraconophobia* (the fear of shellfish). These guys are big but want nothing to do with you, and no, you don't eat them.

Try this. Wait till your friend is recovering from too much ganja and rum, lift one gently from behind the shell, and toss it into your hotel room. Have a camera handy. The sound of large, crabby legs skittering across the floor always elicits a major reaction. Tick tick tick. Wait for the scream.

MEAN LITTLE MASKITTAS

Maskittas (or mosquitoes) are a problem in Jamaica, as they are in much of the Caribbean and the world. Dengue fever is around many of the islands, and Jamaica has its share of problems with this pesky mini-vampire. A bigger problem in the south of Kingston, as large bodies of stagnant water and trash build up to form breeding grounds. You should have some good bug spray around. Bring it with you if you can, as it's very expensive on the island. Bugs do fly, and in parts of Jamaica, they can be so thick that residents are in the house before evening. Government programs to eliminate standing water where the mosquitoes breed are ongoing. Usually, the ocean breeze is enough to keep them away, and the problem does not seem endemic around Negril. October appears to be a bad mosquito month because of the rainy season. You can tell a dengue-carrying mosquito, *Aedes aegypti*, because it has tigerlike stripes on its wings and legs, but try to avoid all mosquitoes anyway.

NO-SEE-UMS

That's what we've always called them, these sand fleas and other tiny guys that are right there to munch on your legs and arms just when you thought you were going to relax with a beer on the beach. Instead, you're being eaten alive, and you can't even see the little killers. Best advice here is to buy Avon's Skin So Soft bug wipes at home and drag the handy little towelettes with you.

They actually seem to work and won't leave you smelling like a duck hunter. I give away my supply to a suffering soul every time;

bring the whole box if insects already seem to have a natural liking for you. You know who you are.

WATTA SPORTS

Negril is blessed with beautiful, protected waters, and the Caribbean Sea becomes an experiment in fun when you let yourself get swept away in its breaking, blue, foamy waves. If you can do it in the water, then you can do it here. Water sports from deep-sea fishing, to going out with local guides in small boats, to tossing a rod by the shore, to Jet-Skis and parasails: these options are everywhere along the beach, and plenty of guys want to give you a ride. Scuba divers here are rewarded with protected, beautiful reefs to visit, and the snorkeling is easy with close and colorful shallow corals that can be explored at your unhurried leisure. All the major and many smaller resorts can get you PADI-certified in time for some great dive adventures around the island. Bring your snorkel gear from home and save on the cost of renting equipment.

You can find yourself floating around on kayaks, windsurfers, rafts, and boats of all descriptions. Catamaran trips are very popular here, and you will often see the catamaran

Wild Thing cruising up and down the coast with loads of happy party animals going down the water slide on the boat and drinking in the bliss. Wild Thing Tours will pick you up at your hotel, so there's no excuse not to get silly once in a while. You'll have a blast on any crazy boat ride around here, as they are designed for pure fun. Visit www.wildthingwatersportsnegril.com for more information.

Whatever you are looking for in the way of water fun and entertainment can be found in and around Seven Mile Beach. Help the local economy, and you'll almost always have a better time with the services provided by vendors up and down the beach. You can always negotiate a better price than most resort excursions. It's true that the water gods have blessed this part of the island, so soak yourself near the seashore and let the sun heat your inner core. Then roll over and take a sip of that Dirty Banana while you become a true believer in the astoundingly chillin' place that is Negril. See you in Jamaica!

ABOUT THIS BOOK!

In case you're wondering, this book is a complete work of insanity and love for Jamaica. I have made several extra trips to Negril with the excuse of needing better photographs for the book, and it could be one of my better scams, but no one in this book has compensated me in any way for any reviews or information in this book—it's all my opinion. I want to thank the people at Createspace.com and Amazon.com for their patience with a happy amateur like myself who has no credentials on the wall certifying me to be a writer of travel guides.

But as a countryman once said, "You just have to have the intention."

Made in the USA
Monee, IL
29 January 2020